"Each chapter is rich with raw i. important discussion of sensitive matters. I cannot imagine a more in-depth, relevant and vital source for parents and grandparents."

—Alan Haas, President
Educational Futures
New Canaan, CT

"Pritchard has given us the "A to Z" of 529 plans. The book is written in clear, lucid prose and is organized in a way that makes answers to specific questions easy to find, while allowing a serious reader to dive deeply into any dimension of these valuable vehicles for college savings."

—Richard Ekman, President
The Council of Independent Colleges
Washington, DC

"I highly recommend this handbook for grandparents. It's easy to read and filled with information that will help you understand the different types of plans, and how you can help your grandchildren achieve a better future."

—Betty Lochner, Director Emeritus
Washington State 529 Plans
Olympia, WA

"Timely and comprehensive book that will help families save efficiently for higher education."

—Paul Curley, CFA
Director of College Savings Research at Strategic Insight
New York, NY

"As a parent, a 529 plan was instrumental in allowing us to focus on the most important aspect of higher education—the right fit. Pritchard's guidebook is a vital resource."

—Hamilton Gregg M. Ed, CEP, Board Member
Higher Education Consultants Association
Beijing, China

"Pritchard has tapped into the power of extended families to show us the critical role that grandparents can play in making their grandkid's college dreams a reality. I recommend this book to my families because Pritchard's financial and familial insights should not to be missed by parents and grandparents who are interested in securing their family's legacy."

—David Montesano
College Admission Strategist
Seattle, WA

"Every dollar saved is one less dollar your grandchildren have to borrow."

—Mitch Seabaugh, Executive Director
Georgia's Path2College 529 Plan
Atlanta, GA

"Run, don't walk, to open a 529 for your grandchild. This detailed book shows how compounding and 529 accounts can be a powerful combination."

—Steven Roy Goodman, MS, JD, CEP
College Admissions Consultant & Author
Washington, DC

"If you are a financial advisor that works with wealthy families who are looking to use educational funding as another valuable wealth transfer technique, you must read this book."

—Allyn Hughes, CFP®, ChFC®, CLU®, CAP®
Brooks, Hughes and Jones
Gig Harbor, WA

"Pritchard's book identifies, in great clarity, the wonderful opportunity 529 plans afford grandparents to pass along the legacy of education to their grandchildren."

—Richard A. Feigenbaum, Esq.
Author of *The 529 College Savings Plan Made Simple*
Wellesley, MA

"Pritchard manages to straddle detailed explanations and concise summaries in a way that makes a complicated subject understandable."

—Lesley Klecan, Board Member
Pacific Northwest Association for College Admission Counseling
Medford, OR

"Pritchard discusses the many benefits 529 plans provide and the important role grandparents can play in creating a family legacy of education."

—Richard J. Polimeni, Chair
College Savings Foundation
Arlington, VA

"An excellent and comprehensive look at purchasing 529 plans for grandchildren."

—Mandee Heller Adler, Founder and CEO
International College Counselors
Author of: *International Admissions: How to get accepted to US Colleges*

"An excellent resource to inspire grandparents to fund 529 plans and create an amazing legacy."

—Jason Parker, CRFA®, RICP®
Author of *Sound Retirement Planning* & Host of *Sound Retirement Radio*
Poulsbo, WA

"A valuable reference work for practitioners."

—Drake Zimmerman, JD, CFA, CFP®, CAP®
Zimmerman & Armstrong Investment Advisors, Inc.
Normal, IL

"Great book for all Grandparents looking to help their grandchildren pay for college."

—Chris Featherstone, CFP® ChFC, Principal
Madison Park Capital Advisors, LLC
Seattle, WA

Other books by Jeffrey J. Pritchard

Low-Risk, High-Performance: Investing with
Convertible Bonds

•

Heads You Win, Tails You Win: The Inside
Secrets to Rare Coin Investing

•

One Trillion to One: The Great Inflations

•

Quest for the Pillars of Wealth: A Children's Guide
To Growing Rich
(middle reader fiction)

•

The Secret Treasures of Oak Island
(middle reader fiction)

•

The Seventh Jewel
(young adult fiction)

529

COLLEGE SAVINGS PLANS
for GRANDPARENTS

Todd —

To a great
investment manager!

529

COLLEGE SAVINGS PLANS
for GRANDPARENTS

Creating a Family Legacy of Higher Education

2019-2020 Edition

Jeffrey J. Pritchard, CFP®, CAP®

© 2019

For permission requests, please address:
Heritage Press
PO Box 10771
Bainbridge Island, WA 98110

Published 2019 by Heritage Press
Printed in the United States of America

21 20 19 18   1 2 3 4
ISBN 978-0-692-15968-2
Library of Congress Control Number: 2018956908

DISCLAIMER

To Amanda

Special thanks and appreciation to
Corinne Cavanaugh - Kathryn Decker, JD
Allyn Hughes, ChFC, CFP®, CAP®, CLU
Drake Zimmerman, JD, CFA, CFP®, CAP®

"Education is the great engine of personal development. It is through education that the daughter of a peasant can become a doctor, that the son of a mineworker can become head of the mine, that a child of farmworkers can become the president of a great nation."

—*Nelson Mandela*

TABLE OF CONTENTS

WHY READ THIS BOOK?

Four thousand years ago Egyptian scribes instructed the young in matters of mathematics, medicine, and geometry. Millennia later Incan temple priests taught future nobility in religion, geography, and astronomy. From civilization's earliest days, education has been necessary for the transmission of society's cultural values and accumulated knowledge. Yet in those times, formal education was the exclusive domain for the most privileged, the wealthiest, and the most politically connected in the highest echelons of society.

But much has changed. College has become essential for more than a few exclusive professions, such as law or medicine. A higher education is indispensable for countless careers and job opportunities, in addition to the timeless value of helping prepare young adults to become responsible and productive citizens. And college is no longer only for the elite. Higher education today, whether a two-year associate's degree, four-year bachelor's degree, or advanced graduate studies, is well within the grasp of every U.S. citizen. Yet herein lies the dilemma: While college as an institution has become democratized and diverse, it is accompanied by a steep price tag.

A single year at a private four-year university, including tuition, fees, and room and board, can easily cost above $65,000, and tuition prices seem to increase every year. A four-year degree at a private college comes with a retail sticker price of $260,000.

Today, students and families face a high-stakes balancing act—weighing the necessity of higher education with the cost of a decades-long financial burden.

529 PLANS

Despite widespread recognition of both the value of higher education and its ever-escalating price, surprisingly few adults are even aware of 529 plans—what they are, how they work, and how they ease the financial burden of college. A recent survey[1] indicates that less than one-third of adults are familiar with them, and the 529 recognition level declines with the age of the survey respondents. So, what are 529 plans?

A 529 plan is a tax-advantaged saving plan created under the Small Business Job Protection Act of 1996 and is specifically defined in Section 529 of the Internal Revenue Code. The plans, officially called qualified tuition programs, are meant to encourage saving for postsecondary education, be that training from a vocational trade school, a Ph.D. from an Ivy League university, or anything in between. Individual savings plans are sponsored by the states, state agencies, or educational institutions.

There are three types of 529 plans. Forty-nine states, plus the District of Columbia, offer at least one type of plan, while many states offer all three. Most states also offer state income tax deductions for contributions made to their 529 plans.

---

[1] ORC International's CARAVAN Omnibus Surveys, "529 Plan Awareness Survey," Edward Jones, May 17, 2018, *www.edwardjones.com*.

Prepaid tuition plans: These plans enable a college saver (be that a student, parent, or grandparent) to purchase units or credits for participating colleges and universities (typically in-state public institutions) at today's prices for tomorrow's tuition, even if enrollment is eighteen or twenty years down the road. These usually have residency requirements for either the college saver or the eventual student within the state sponsoring the plan. At the end of 2017, there were 1.1 million prepaid tuition plan holders in the United States containing a combined total of $25 billion.[2]

529 ABLE plans: These plans are the most recent addition to the 529 saving plan options. Created under the Achieving a Better Life Experience Act of 2014 (ABLE), these tax-advantaged savings accounts allow individuals with disabilities to set money aside for educational expenses, or other expenses related to their disability, without being disqualified from government programs, such as Medicaid.

While ABLE plans are administered at the state level, there are no state residency requirements to participate. As of December 31, 2017, there were a little over 17,000 529 ABLE accounts holding $48.5 million in assets.[3]

College Savings Plans: These plans are the most flexible and popular of the three 529 options. This option allows a college saver/ account owner to establish an investment fund to help pay a student's or a beneficiary's qualified higher education expenses. Qualified expenses not only include tuition and mandatory school fees, but also textbooks, computers, and room and board. Withdrawals can be used at virtually any college or university in the United States, as well as a large number of overseas institutions.

---

[2] Curley, Paul, "529 College Savings & ABLE, Data Highlights: 4Q 2017," Strategic Insight, February 18, 2018, *www.sionline.com*.

[3] Ibid.

The account owner/saver can typically select from a broad spectrum of investment options. Most importantly, any capital gains, dividends, or interest accumulating over the life of the account can be withdrawn completely tax-free for the aforementioned qualified education expenses. While 529 savings plans are administered by individual states, unlike prepaid tuition plans, there are normally no in-state residence requirements.

As mentioned, college savings plans are easily the most popular 529 vehicle. At the close of 2017, they contained $294 billion in investments held in 12.3 million accounts.[4] That's a far cry from the $2.4 billion held in the savings plans at the end of 1996.[5]

Due to the wide array of tax-free investment options, limited in-state residency requirements, a broad menu of qualifying expenses, and numerous other appealing characteristics, 529 college savings plans are the primary focus of this book and the ideal way for grandparents to establish a family tradition of higher education support.

WHY GRANDPARENTS?

Virtually all articles, surveys, books, and blogs offering advice on how to finance a college education are directed toward students or their parents. Yet that neglects what may be the most important constituency. It's actually grandparents who are often best positioned to provide meaningful financial assistance at the optimum time period to support their grandchildren's eventual career aspirations. Additionally, as heads of their respective families, grandparents have the stature to provide advice and encouragement to their grandchildren about attending college, thereby laying the foundation for an enduring family educational legacy.

[4] Ibid.

[5] 529 Report: An Exclusive Year-End Review of 529 Plan Activity, The College Savings Plans Network, March 2015, *www.collegesavings.org*.

Saving early: The best time in life for parents to set aside savings for their children's education, due to the power of long-term investment compounding, is when those children are babies. However, this is typically the most difficult time to save as parents are still in the earlier stages of their careers, may be saving to purchase a home, and are bearing the cost of all those diapers! It's a challenging time to save. Fidelity's tenth edition of its College Savings Indicator Survey reported that 71 percent of parents had not attained their college savings goals by the time their children reached college age.[6] That savings shortfall probably explains why in another research study, 44 percent of parents said they felt guilty that they hadn't been able to save more and, perhaps to compensate, 37 percent of all parents surveyed in the same study were considering borrowing from their own retirement savings to assist their children with college.[7] Many grandparents, on the other hand, have by this time substantially benefited from decades of compounded investment growth.

Upper middle-class squeeze: If both parental spouses are working, total household income can easily exceed $100,000. At this level, the availability of grants and aid for college materially declines, requiring parents to bear a larger and larger portion of their children's tuition burden. According to a 2017 survey by Sallie Mae (formerly the Student Loan Marketing Association),[8] on average across all income levels, parents paid 23 percent of their children's tuition costs, with the balance coming from loans, grants, and student payments. However, when household income passed the $100,000 threshold,

---

[6] "10-Year College Progress Report: Fidelity Finds Record-High Number of Families Saving and Investing in 529 Plans," Fidelity Investments, August 25, 2016, *www.fidelity.com*.

[7] Pentis, Andrew, "Survey: 44% of Parents Feel Guilty about Not Saving Enough for College," Student Loan Hero, May 15, 2018, *www.studentloanhero.com*.

[8] Sallie Mae and Ipsos Public Affairs, *How America Pays for College – 2017: Sallie Mae's National Study of College Students and Parents*, 2017, *www.SallieMae.com/HowAmericaPaysforCollege*.

the parental portion of college funding rose to 38 percent, primarily due to a decrease in the availability of grants and federally subsidized loans.

GRANDPARENTS HAVE HAD TIME ON THEIR SIDE: A great many grandparents have been able to financially benefit from long-term compound growth of their investments. Whether this fortuitous situation is the result of hard work and discipline, initiative and entrepreneurship, foresight and wisdom, or just plain dumb luck, grandparents are often in a much stronger financial position at the time of their grandchildren's birth than their grandchildren's parents. Individuals in the U.S. aged 55 or older own 64 percent of all assets while persons under the age of 35 own a mere 3 percent.[9]

ENJOY YOUR GIFT'S IMPACT: One of the greatest benefits of giving to your grandchildren's education while you're still alive, as opposed to a gift from your estate, is that you can enjoy and experience the positive impact of your gift. You can watch them select their school, listen to their enthusiastic college stories when they're home on break, and even receive their justified appreciation of your support. Gifts made to your loved ones during your lifetime are much more joyous and fulfilling.

CREATING AN EDUCATIONAL LEGACY: This is by far the most important reason this book is directed towards grandparents. Grandparents have an opportunity to create a lasting family tradition of encouraging and financially assisting future generations' pursuit of higher education. Education represents a very personal and special gift from grandparent to grandchild that will be long remembered, even to the time when a grandparent's grandchildren become grand

---

[9] "Distribution of Wealth in US by Age," Free By 50, September 6, 2012, *www. freeby50.com.*

parents in their own right. An educational legacy creates a family touchstone for future generations.

The underlying purpose of this book is to urge grandparents to consider creating or continuing a family legacy of higher education support, to underscore the financial and character-building advantages of postsecondary education, and to explore in detail 529 college savings plans, the most efficient way of financially supporting your grandchildren's college aspirations.

Chapter 1

THE IMPORTANCE OF FAMILY LEGACY

We all appreciate the joy that grandchildren bring grandparents. They enrich our lives with unconditional love, boundless energy, unbridled optimism, and happiness. Grandchildren enable grandparents to reconnect with their children. Perhaps most importantly, grandchildren can provide a reassuring sense that our own lives have had meaning and purpose as we reflect on the circular rhythm of generations.

But conversely, grandparents play important roles in the lives of their grandchildren. Grandparents can be inspirational heroes for having struggled and survived through adversity, be that wars, financial hardship, social injustice, or personal sacrifice, as well as being admired for their accomplishments. Additionally, insulated from the day-to-day distractions of parenthood and parental discipline, grandparents can be a special friend and close confidant to their grandchildren.

Grandparents may also provide a stable role model for their grandchildren, as some parents are unable to spend significant time with their children due to job constraints, divorce, even incarceration. Grandparents can offer an emotional and social safety net that can make vulnerable grandchildren feel a little safer, a little more secure.

But perhaps the most important role for grandparents, and the one most relevant to the subject matter of this book, is that of family historian, a champion of the stories, traditions, and legacies that define who the family is with respect to the rest of society. Grandparents can keep the flame of traditions burning so they will be cherished when it's time for the torch to be passed.

Family history is important in the lives of our grandchildren. It defines who we are, what makes our family unique and, in turn, what makes them unique. Family stories and history create a connection to past generations, a solid grounding, and a strong foundation for the next generation.

Perhaps this is expressed most eloquently in *You Can Go Home Again: Reconnecting with Your Family* by Monica McGoldrick:

> We are born not just into our family, but into our family's stories, which both nourish and sometimes cripple us. And when we die, the stories of our lives become part of our family's web of meaning. Family stories tend to be told to remind members of the family's cherished beliefs. We sing of the heroes and even the villains whose daring the family admires.

GRANDPARENTS AND FAMILY VALUES

A legacy is commonly defined as "anything handed down from the past, as from an ancestor, or predecessor."[1] All too often, we think of a legacy in terms of cash, or securities, or real estate, or even personal property. Yet I believe the most valuable legacy you can bestow upon your grandchildren is the gift of encouragement and financial support in their pursuit of higher education—be that a four-year college degree or two-year associate's degree. And to do so reinforces that your encouragement and support is a bedrock family tradition.

---

[1] *Dictionary.com, LLC, www.dictionary.com.*

While our basic family traditions are meaningful and defining, such as specific recipes at Thanksgiving or all watching the same nostalgic movie every Christmas or Hanukkah, creating or maintaining a legacy of higher education is deeper, more impactful, with transformative potential for current grandchildren and future generations as well.

A legacy of education helps clarify your family values and helps grandchildren define themselves. Think of all the empowering messages an educational legacy or family tradition of college support conveys to your grandchildren about your family, about themselves, even about you, their grandparent:

- Our family believes education is important

- We believe in the promise of the future and of your generation

- You're worth our investment in you

- We encourage and support your pursuing your dreams and passions

- Higher education is simply part of becoming an adult

- We want you to develop your knowledge, your talents, and your values

- Our family looks forward to the future—not backward

A family tradition of higher education can also mollify an age-old generational conflict. As long as there have been families, there has been tension. This is particularly true among teenage family members, between being their own individual person but at the same time being part of the family whole. A tradition of encouragement and support of higher education may be the best solution for this dilemma. The underlying tradition itself promotes a sense of community and group values, while at the same time, college promotes each grandchild's individual personal development. A college education sends the message that we want you to lead your own life, while staying connected to the family and its traditions.

KEY CHAPTER TAKEAWAYS

- Sustaining family traditions is a critical role for grandparents
- Creating a pathway to higher education can be the most important legacy grandparents leave their heirs

Chapter 2

THE GREATEST GIFT

A college degree's most obvious benefit is in preparing your grandchildren for a successful career in their chosen field of study. The monetary value, or financial return on an investment in tuition, is thoroughly explored in Chapter 5. The following pages explain the intangible benefits of a college education, beyond the confines of career preparation, and how those intangible factors can positively impact the development and growth of your grandchildren.

NEW OPPORTUNITIES

A college degree has the potential to open previously unknown doors of opportunity. College provides exposure and access to new and exciting fields of study, it embeds grandchildren into a network of energetic fellow students, and allows mentoring by thought leaders in their respective fields. In today's world, fair or not, a college degree is the admission ticket to some of the most exciting and meaningful opportunities. Your grandchildren are competing internationally in a knowledge-based world. The surest pathway to participate and thrive in the new economy is through higher education.

Additionally, college education has played, and continues to play, a vital role in opening doors of opportunity for women and minorities, helping overcome the last remnants of institutional discrimination, be it conscious or unconscious.

A BROADER WORLD VIEW

Despite the increasing diversity of our nation, many young people grow up in a house of mirrors or echo chamber. Most of their friends look like them, come from a similar socio-economic level, hold similar political or world views, have a similar lifestyle, and even share similar goals. For many young people, college is the first point in which they must closely associate, socialize, room, and truly listen to fellow students from different countries, cultures, races, and backgrounds. Each of them come with their own set of preconceived beliefs and biases. Your grandchildren may initially believe they have nothing in common with these students.

College can also be the first time students must critically examine their own views, while thoughtfully and objectively considering the views and perspectives of others. That can be profound. Exposure and engagement with a wide variety of peoples instill a more balanced and worldly view, a greater sense of tolerance for those who are different, a more thoughtful, less reactionary response to opposing viewpoints, and the ability to think beyond the narrow confines of themselves.

CIVIC ENGAGEMENT

Numerous studies attest to the fact that higher education in the United States creates a more informed and involved citizenry, greatly increasing the odds of your grandchildren becoming engaged and supportive community participants.

Perhaps the simplest indicator of civic engagement is voting. The College Board reported that in the 2012 general election, among 25–44 year-old adults, 42 percent of high school only adults voted, 58 percent of those holding associate's degrees, and 73 percent for those with bachelor's degrees. That same trend held during the 2014 mid-term elections as well. The voting rate for those with bachelor's degrees (45 percent) was more than twice as high as the voting rate for high school graduates (only 20 percent).[1]

In terms of volunteering for the betterment of the community by individuals twenty-five years old and above, of those with no post-secondary education only 16 percent reported volunteering in 2015, compared with 27 percent of those with some college or an associate's degree, while 39 percent of those with a bachelor's degree or higher reported volunteering.

A college education acts as an incubator of civic engagement, responsibility, and philanthropy with graduates more committed to a just and equitable community.

HEALTHIER GRANDCHILDREN

The long-term health benefits for your grandchildren probably don't jump out as incentives for you to encourage and assist them to attend college. However, higher education is correlated with healthier lifestyles.[2]

- Smoking—During 2014, among adults twenty-five years old and older, only 8 percent of individuals with a bachelor's degree smoked, compared to 20 percent for those

---

[1] Ma, Jennifer; Pender, Matea; Welch, Meredith. *Education Pays 2016 – The Benefits of Education for Individuals and Society.* Boston: The College Board, 2016.

[2] Ibid.

with some college or an associate's degree, while 26 percent of those with only a high school diploma smoked. And this smoking/education gap has steadily widened over the past few decades.

- Obesity—Obesity has become a serious health problem in America. During the last twenty years, the obesity rate has dramatically risen across all sectors of the population. Yet the higher an individual's level of education, the less likely they are to become obese.

  The relationship between obesity and less education is most likely due to income differentials, dietary knowledge, and the price of healthier foods, but all those are encompassed in the advantages of education.

- Exercise—Even an individual's exercise is influenced by education. Adults with a high school diploma reported lower rates of weekly exercise than those with a bachelor's degree, and the exercise/education gap increased with age.

CONFIDENCE AND DISCIPLINE

After completing the many degree requirements, having spent years of dedicated and disciplined study, pushing themselves beyond what they might have originally thought possible, college graduation instills in individuals a very real and justified sense of accomplishment, not to mention the impact of any awards, special recognition, publications, and athletic or artistic achievements they may have garnered along the way.

Completing college is an accomplishment that imbues a greater sense of pride, self-esteem, and self-confidence. A graduating grandchild brimming with confidence has a greater sense of what's possible and of what they can go on to accomplish in the work world. That alone is an invaluable gift to your grandchildren.

EXCELLENCE

College surrounds your grandchildren with the best and the brightest, other smart, intellectually curious young adults striving to excel in their respective fields of endeavor. It is an environment that motivates and inspires your grandchildren to excel as well, to be the best they can be.

An acquaintance of mine, a senior partner in a law firm, once remarked that the most valuable thing about a law degree was that it trained students how to think. Regardless of what road they then chose to take after law school, they now possessed the ability to think critically, to ask questions, to analyze, reflect, to logically approach complex problems—invaluable lifelong skills both professionally and personally.

A rigorous college education encourages students to think logically and critically and to approach old problems in new creative ways. College sharpens a student's ability to grasp and explain abstract theories and concepts, and to express themselves clearly in both speech and in writing.

ENSURING THE FUTURE

All of our families are part of something bigger. Higher education's importance reaches beyond individual grandchildren and beyond our family legacies and traditions. If the United States is to remain the leader, or a leader, in twenty-first century technology, along with the requisite workforce to accompany it, a highly educated population is critical. If we are to have a fair and just society in which upward mobility is a possibility for all Americans and not the favored few, then higher education is critical. If we are to have a free and prosperous democracy in which an informed citizenry is committed to democracy's ideals and responsibilities, then higher education is critical. And if we are to successfully pass all that we cherish to future generations, and to trust in their stewardship, then higher education is critical. President Franklin D. Roosevelt observed, "The real safeguard of democracy is education."

THE ENDURING GIFT

Finally, imagine all the tangible gifts you could bestow upon your grandchildren: large sums of money, stock of the company you founded, the family vacation home, a prized piece of real estate, or perhaps family possessions handed down from earlier generations. But in reality, these generous inheritances may be fleeting. Money can be squandered, a vacation home can burn down, securities can collapse amid economic turmoil, family keepsakes can be lost or stolen. And any of the treasured assets passed to grandchildren can be lost or diminished through divorce or bankruptcy. Education is the gift that endures. It remains amid economic calamity or declining health. It can survive the ravages of war, and its portability transcends borders and boundaries. It cannot be lost, stolen, or given away. It always remains a core component of your grandchild's essence—and a bedrock family legacy.

KEY CHAPTER TAKEAWAYS

- Postsecondary education can be transformational for grandchildren

  - Provides new opportunities

  - Fosters tolerance through a broader world view

  - Enhances their civic engagement

  - Strengthens self-confidence and discipline

  - Can spur your grandchildren to excel

Chapter 3

HISTORY AND BACKGROUND

Back in the mid-1980s when I began saving for my own children's college education, there weren't a lot of great options. A common method for parental financial support was to gift assets (cash, stocks, bonds) to children via the Uniform Gifts to Minors Act (UGMA). This provided a modest tax break and earmarked those funds as belonging to your children, preferably for college. But looking back, the approach had more negatives than positives.

First, those gifts to my children were permanent. The moment they were transferred, they became their property. I could still oversee the assets, but if I had a financial emergency, retrieving those assets was difficult to impossible. And once children reached the wise old age of eighteen in the state of Washington, they could do whatever they desired with the funds. Second, the tax break was also thin. Once those assets earned beyond a modest level of income, earnings were taxed at the parents' highest tax rate. (This is affectionately known as the kiddie tax.)

To top things off, since the students actually owned those assets, they were heavily weighted in computations for grant or scholarship qualification. In a perverse manner, my best intentions may have actually impaired my children's ability to obtain the same grants or scholarships available to their classmates. All that officially changed for the better in 1996.

A Visionary Idea

The first suggestion of a state-based financial instrument to assist families with college tuition is credited to Michigan Governor James J. Blanchard. During his state of the state address in January 1986, he articulated his vision for a prepaid tuition program that would "help parents guarantee their children the opportunity of a Michigan college education."[1] While more than a dozen private colleges had previously used a prepaid tuition concept, this was the first time it had been proposed for the general public.[2]

Governor Blanchard's insightful proposal became the Michigan Education Trust (MET). "By using the combined investment power of Michigan, a higher interest rate can be earned and compounded without taxation," said Blanchard. "This program will guarantee to pay a child's tuition, whatever the cost might be by the time the child enters college."[3] However, the state postponed initial rollout pending an IRS ruling on the program's tax treatment.

The IRS response wasn't encouraging. It ruled that Michigan had to pay tax each year on any realized investment gains occurring within the trust. That factor alone made keeping up with tuition inflation a challenge. But the IRS added that when the student beneficiary finally utilized those prepaid tuition credits, they would be fully taxed

---

[1] Hurley, Joseph, *The Best Way to Save for College: A Complete Guide to 529 Plans*, SavingforCollege.com Publications, 2015.

[2] Barron, James, "Education: Michigan Plan Guarantees College Tuition," *The New York Times*, December 30, 1986.

[3] Barron, James, "Michigan Governor to Urge College Tuition Guarantee," *The New York Times*, January 29, 1986.

on the increased price of tuition, as if the plan was some sort of stand-alone investment. In reality, the students would have been taxed on tuition inflation. Ouch! This double taxation severely restricted the potential of Blanchard's original vision. Michigan proceeded with MET but sued the IRS.

In 1990, Michigan filed a lawsuit against the IRS demanding a refund of all taxes paid on behalf of the MET program up to that point in time. The district court ruled in favor of the IRS. In 1994, upon Michigan's appeal, the appellate court ruled in favor of the state. The IRS then considered challenging each state individually in court, determined to retain tuition taxes collected under other state's programs.

IRS intransigence combined with the possibility of protracted state-by-state legal skirmishes thrust college savings programs into the limelight of the Small Business Jobs Protection Act of 1996. Spearheaded by Bob Graham of Florida and Mitch McConnell of Kentucky, this legislation created Section 529 of the Internal Revenue Code, which deals with qualified tuition programs.

The legislation formally shielded 529 college plan investments from taxation while held by the state, and any taxation to the student beneficiary was deferred until the funds were used for education. Thus, college savings plans and other qualified tuition plans under Internal Revenue Code Section 529 were officially born; however, they still had a long way to evolve.

ENHANCED FEATURES

In 2001, as part of President Bush's Economic Growth and Tax Relief Reconciliation Act (EGTRRA), college savings plans were significantly expanded. Recognizing the need to provide more comprehensive financial relief for families with college-bound students, the legislation contained the following enhancements:

TAXES: Most importantly, the EGTRRA legislation granted full tax-exempt status to 529 plan investment earnings ultimately used for qualified education expenses. This was the same provision President Clinton vetoed just four years earlier when it was originally part of the Taxpayers Relief Act of 1997. Previously, the earnings portion of distributions were taxed at the beneficiary's (student's) full income tax rate. While this was inevitably lower than the parents' rate of taxation, the tax-free aspect was a huge leap forward.

EXPENSES: Prior to 2001, a student's annual qualified housing expenses were limited to either $1,500 if they were living at home; dormitory expenses if living on campus; or $2,500 per year if the student was living in noncampus housing. The legislation increased qualified off-campus housing expenses to be on a par with campus dormitory expense levels.

ROLLOVERS: 529 account owners were now permitted to roll over or transfer account funds from one 529 plan to another without tax consequences, so long as the accounts had the same student beneficiary.

FAMILY: The legislation also expanded the definition of family to include first cousins for the purpose of changing an account's named beneficiary. Previously, changing the account's beneficiary to a first cousin of the original beneficiary was viewed as a nonqualified distribution, with the accompanying tax on earnings and 10 percent penalty.

SPECIAL NEEDS: A precursor to the disabilities-related 529 provisions of 2014, qualified educational expenses could now include costs for special needs services necessary for a special needs beneficiary to attend school.

THE CINDERELLA CLAUSE

The 529 plan improvements from 2001 were well received by the public, educators, and even by financial advisors. But there was a catch! All the enhancements referenced above would expire at the stroke of midnight on December 31, 2010, like many of the other provisions within EGTRRA.

The legislation's sunset provision created a financial time bomb for parents or grandparents with long-term college funding plans. A couple dutifully saving within a 529 plan for a grandchild's education with the expectation of tax-free growth would be more than a little irritated if upon distribution for tuition purposes, they discovered that feature had expired. The possibility of eventually owing taxes created a disincentive to open 529 plans for grandchildren if they would need the funds after the 2010 deadline.

To remedy this and other tax uncertainties, on August 17, 2006, President Bush signed the Pension Protection Act (PPA) of 2006. As the name implies, the underlying intent of the legislation was to strengthen and protect workers' pension and retirement plans, many of which were, and still are, woefully underfunded with respect to their contractual obligations. Among other features, PPA made the 529 plan enhancements from five years earlier permanent. They would no longer expire at the end of 2010.

With tax uncertainties eliminated, college savings plan contributions jumped. During 2007, the first full year after the PPA legislation went into effect, 529 account balances increased 20 percent to $148.6 billion.[4] In contrast, during that same period, the financial markets, as measured by the S&P 500 Index, actually declined 3 percent.

---

[4] Hannon, Simona; Moore, Kevin; Schmeiser, Max; Stefanescu, Irina; "Saving for College and Section 529 Plans," FEDS Notes, February 3, 2016, *www.federalreserve. gov.*

SPECIAL CONSIDERATIONS

On December 19, 2014, President Obama signed the Achieving a Better Life Experience (ABLE) Act into law. As detailed in Chapter 15, the ABLE Act represented a major step forward in support of individuals with disabilities and special needs. The law enabled families to contribute to a 529 ABLE account opened on behalf of a family member with special needs, and the funds could then appreciate on a tax-free basis like a traditional 529 savings plan. More importantly, the first $100,000 in the account would no longer disqualify the beneficiary from receiving Supplemental Security Income as it would have in the past. Previously, this point created a significant disincentive to save.

The ABLE Act also positively impacted traditional 529 savings plans. Prior to 2014, a 529 account owner could only change their investment portfolio once per year (unless they were changing the beneficiary). The ABLE Act allowed for two investment changes per year.

PUBLIC SUPPORT

The clearest indicator of the widespread and bipartisan political support 529 savings plans had attained in their brief history occurred in early-2015. In January of that year, President Obama floated the idea of eliminating tax-exempt status for 529 savings plans. The resulting tax revenue was to help pay for another of his proposals—free community college for everyone.

The 529 portion of his proposal met an immediate firestorm from both political parties. Some of the harshest opposition came from Obama's own party. Speaker of the House Nancy Pelosi, a fellow Democrat, pointedly lobbied administrative officials while aboard Air Force One to abandon the idea of taxing 529 savings plans.[5]

---

[5] Stratford, Michael, "Politics of the 529 Plan," News, Inside Higher Ed, January 29, 2015, *www.insidehighered.com.*

The administration had portrayed 529 plans as a savings instrument only benefitting the very rich. However, families across the demographic spectrum benefitted from the tax-advantaged programs and felt they were an important part of their college financing toolbox. The College Savings Foundation pointed out at the time that "close to 10 percent of 529 account holders have incomes below $50,000, and more than 70 percent of the total number of accounts are owned by households with incomes below $150,000."[6]

Within days of first floating the proposal, President Obama quietly withdrew it. At the time, a prominent educator referred to 529 college savings plans as a new "third rail issue,"[7] enjoying such widespread public and political support that dramatically modifying the program, let alone eliminating it, was all but impossible. That put 529 plans on an equal footing with Social Security or individual retirement accounts in that it would be exceedingly difficult to roll back benefits.

The incident illustrates how engrained the 529 program has become with families saving for postsecondary education and the ensuing widespread political support.

QUALIFIED SCHOOLS

The most recent legislative expansion of 529 plans was an eleventh-hour addition to the Tax Cuts and Jobs Act in late-2017. The legislation broadened the definition of qualified educational expenses to include kindergarten through twelfth grade private tuition up to $10,000 per year.

---

[6] Gibson, Cary, "Obama's 529 Missteps, The President Erred When he Proposed Taxing College Savings Plans," *US News*, February 2, 2015, *www.usnews.com*.

[7] The third rail refers to the additional rail in a subway system that carries high electrical current to power the trains. Touching the third rail is fatal. Politicians adopted the term to describe an issue too controversial to discuss.

This particular 529 enhancement turned out to be extremely controversial. The amendment was criticized in that those utilizing the K-12 exemption probably wouldn't financially need it. Additionally, the financial planning community balked at the prospect of families prematurely dipping into their college savings plans and thereby forgoing years of tax-free compounding on the withdrawn funds. The K-12 question is examined more thoroughly in Chapter 12.

College savings plans originally sanctioned under Section 529 of the Internal Revenue Code have come a long way since Governor Blanchard first proposed the concept back in 1986. Today, 529 plans represent the most flexible and advantageous method for grandparents to assist their grandchildren in pursuit of their educational aspirations.

KEY CHAPTER TAKEAWAYS

- Since their official inception in 1996, 529 college savings plans have evolved into the most efficient way to save for college

- Despite political push and pull, the vast majority of both the public and politicians, support 529 savings plans

Chapter 4

THE RISING COST OF COLLEGE
(Why your grandchild could use a helping hand!)

T omorrow's college student faces a daunting financial challenge because of the declining affordability of a postsecondary education. Four components create the perfect storm in terms of the rising cost of college.

RISING TUITION

Can you remember a time when college wasn't considered expensive? When it wasn't a financial sacrifice for or a burden on most families? The fact is, postsecondary education has always been expensive. Yet that financial burden has become heavier in recent years. It's the obvious reason that your grandchildren would welcome, even cherish, any financial assistance you're willing or able to provide in their pursuit of higher education and higher opportunities.

Over the preceding decades, the rising cost of a college education has far exceeded the rate of inflation. Consider Yale University as a case in point. Back in 1939–1940 it cost $900 to attend Yale for one year, including room and board.[1] Adjusted for inflation, that equates to $15,900 in 2018 dollars. But that's not what Yale costs today. Tuition, fees, books, and room and board cost today's students over $65,000. And Yale's rate of tuition increase is not unusual.

According to data compiled by the College Board, tuition and room and board at the average private university is nearly $47,000 per year! More troubling for those yet to enter college, based on the underlying causes of rising college costs, tuition increases will continue for the foreseeable future.

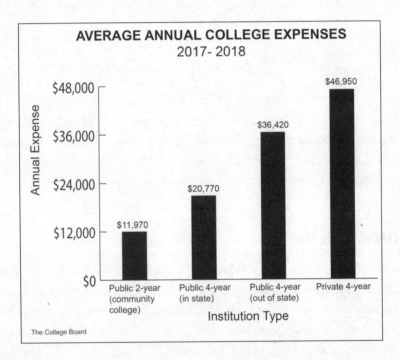

As lofty as these prices are, they're only for a single year. Assuming your grandchildren graduate on time, which is statistically unlikely, the total retail cost of a bachelor's degree at a four-year public school averages $83,000 for in-state students, $145,680 at public schools for

---

[1] Zurolo, Mark, "The Cost of Yale: A History," *Yale Alumni Magazine*, May/June 2015, *www.yalealumnimagazine.com*.

nonresidents, and a whopping $187,800 at the average private four-year university. Ouch! And these prices can be particularly frustrating when one sees the vast sums colleges fundraise from alumni and donors, which totaled $43.6 billion in 2017.[2]

Yet as alarming as these prices appear, if one assumes the upward trend in college tuition continues along the same trajectory they've experienced since 1985, it ensures that many of tomorrow's prospective students will either be priced out of the college education they desire or burdened with a crushing level of student loans. The graph below illustrates past and projected cost of one year of college by category assuming the next ten years mirror the last thirty in the rate of educational tuition inflation.

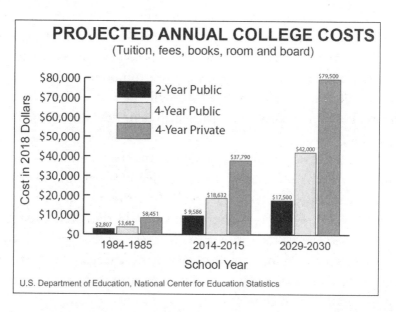

A meaningful discussion of why college costs keep rising faster than core inflation is beyond the scope of this writing. Inflationary tuition factors include administrative staff expanding at a greater rate

---

[2] Goldrick-Rab, Sara; McCluskey, Neal; "Should College Education Be Free?" *The Wall Street Journal*, March 20, 2018.

than student enrollment, an indulgent menu of student services and amenities, a severe decline in state-government funding for public schools, an increase in federal loan availability, and the psychological effect of a school's reputation being enhanced the higher its tuition. (One think tank has suggested 529 plans themselves are partially to blame for rising tuition,[3] an opinion not shared by this author.) Regardless of whether you believe college costs are justified, the reality is that the price of a college education will cost more every year well into the future.

THE RISING COST OF STUDENT DEBT

The long-term burden of student loans will be discussed in Chapter 6. What many pundits overlook, even those who decry student loans the loudest, is that the loan burden will become even heavier for future students. The cost of borrowing those tuition funds, the interest rate on their loans, are set to substantially increase. (This may be a small blessing for those who incurred student debt during the 2008 recession.)

The interest rate on federal student loans is determined at the beginning of each year based on a formula that incorporates two factors: an administrative fee combined with the current yield on ten-year treasury notes. Once a student borrows funds, they are locked into that interest rate for the entire repayment term of their loan, which is typically structured for a ten-year repayment schedule. (Students can consolidate all their annual loans into one at the conclusion of their education if they so choose.)

Student loan rates for the 2018–2019 school year were determined as follows:

---

[3] Reeves, Richard V.; Joo, Nathan; "A Tax Break for Dream Hoarders: What to do about 529 College Savings Plans", Washington DC: Brookings, June 29, 2017

- Undergraduate Student Loans:
  Ten-year Treasury rate of 3.00 percent plus administrative fee of 2.05 percent = 5.05 percent rate

- Graduate Student Loans:
  Ten-year Treasury rate of 3.00 percent plus 3.60 percent administrative fee = 6.6 percent rate

Students who borrow when interest rates are low are relatively fortunate compared to students forced to borrow when interest rates are high.

Since 2011, students have been able to borrow at unusually low interest rates. That's about to change. During the depths of the 2008 recession, the Federal Reserve reduced borrowing rates to historically low levels to spur lending and thereby economic activity. Undergraduate student lending rates declined to 3.40 percent between 2011 and 2013.

However, with the U.S. economy firmly back on track, unemployment at record lows, the Federal Reserve has begun the process of raising interest rates back to more normal levels. As of this writing, the ten-year Treasury yield is 3.0 percent, while the average rate since 1900 has been 4.9 percent. (The ten-year Treasury rate spiked to 15.3 percent during the 1980s.) As interest rates return to historical norms, borrowing rates for students will significantly increase, adding even more to the long-term expense of college.

Table 4.1 below illustrates the increased borrowing cost to students in contrasting the 2018–2019 borrowing rate of 5.05 percent and the maximum student loan allowable rate of 8.25 percent, which was the prevailing rate between 1995 and 1998. It adds a significant amount over the life of the loan!

Table 4.1
Rising interest rate impact on student loan repayment
(All figures based on a standard ten-year repayment)

	Borrowing	Borrowing
$25,000 loan:	at 5.05%	at 8.25%
Monthly payment	$265.78	$306.63
Total interest over loan life	$ 6,893.60	$11,795.79
Total amount paid	$31,893.60	$36,795.79
$100,000 loan:		
Monthly payment	$1,063.11	$1,226.53
Total interest over loan life	$27,572.54	$ 47,183.15
Total amount paid	$127,572.54	$147,183.15

As the low interest rate environment gradually gives way to normal rates, future students needing to borrow will pay a larger and larger portion of their income. One more factor in the rising financial burden of a postsecondary education.

IT'S TAKING LONGER TO GRADUATE

Adding financial insult to injury, students aren't graduating on time. In addition to rising tuition and borrowing costs, odds are it will take your grandchildren longer than four years to attain their four-year bachelor's degree, and longer than two years to earn an associate's degree.

According to a recent study by the National Student Clearinghouse Research Center, evaluating over two million students receiving their bachelor's or associate's degree in the 2014–2015 school year, it takes between five and six years for the average student to complete their four-year program.

The average length of active enrollment for students earning a bachelor's degree from a four-year public institution is 5.2 academic years of full-time-equivalent enrollment stretched out over 5.6 calendar years. Students graduating at four-year private nonprofit institutions took a bit less time: 4.8 academic years covering 5.4 calendar years. Perhaps more troubling, the study found that nearly a quarter of all bachelor degree recipients from all institutions did not finish within six calendar years.

Table 4.2

Enrolled and elapsed time to degree attainment[4]

TYPE OF INSTITUTION	YEARS OF ENROLLED TIME*	YEARS OF ELAPSEDTIME**
2-year public	3.4	5.6
4-year public	5.2	5.6
4-year private (non-profit)	4.8	5.4
4-year private (for profit)	5.8	8.8

*Years of enrolled time equivalent to years of full-time enrollment, thereby adjusting for part-time students.
**Total calendar years from initial enrollment to degree attainment.

Admittedly, averages can be deceiving, covering a wide dispersion of results, which is the case here. The results of the study found that only 37.5 percent (little better than one-third) of students at public four-year colleges were able to complete their degrees in the allotted four-year time period. Over 36 percent of the students at four-year public

---

[4] Shapiro, D., Dundar, A., Wakhunga, P.K., Yuan, X, A, & Hwang. (2016, September). *Time to Degree: A National View of the Time Enrolled and Elapsed for Associate and Bachelor's Degree Earners.* Herndon, VA: National Student Clearinghouse Research Center.

universities took six calendar years or longer to attain their bachelor's degree. And the longer students are in school to receive their degree, the more costs accumulate.

So, why is it taking students longer to graduate? Have they become lazy or dumbed down over the years? Of course not. But a combination of factors, the fault of both students and institutions, have made on-time graduation less common. The most prevalent of these factors, according to a study conducted by Complete College America, include:[5]

- Lack of a clear plan: Freshman enter college with an overly relaxed attitude and a lack of clarity on what will be expected of them academically.

- Insufficient counsel by the institution: New students frequently need sound guidance on the best pathway to degree attainment but often don't receive it.

- Changing majors: The National Center for Education Statistics points out that nearly 80 percent of graduating students change their major prior to receiving their degree.

- Changing schools: The 2016 National Clearinghouse Study found that a whopping 64 percent of all bachelor's degree recipients attended more than one institution prior to degree completion. Classes rarely transfer for full credit from one school to the next, requiring additional classes.

- Taking unnecessary classes: This is related to all of the reasons above. An average bachelor's degree requires 120 credits.[6] Yet according to the Complete College America report, most undergraduate students take a total of 134 credits on the road to attaining their degrees. Since tuition

---

[5] "Common College Completion Metrics Technical Guide," Indianapolis: Complete College America, March 28, 2017.

[6] Ibid.

pricing within an institution is based on the number of credits taken, even if your grandchild graduates in four years by taking an above-average class load, their costs will be higher than advertised.

Each additional term, quarter, semester, or class credit taken invariably increases the underlying cost of college through increased tuition, fees, room and board, and the opportunity cost of delaying their entry into the workforce.

BUT WAIT—WHAT ABOUT ALL THOSE STUDENT GRANTS?

While this book is focused on 529 savings plans as a means of financing a college education, your grandchildren should aggressively seek scholarships and grants from every conceivable source to help defray the cost of their education. And there is a lot of grant money out there.

However, the majority of students at public schools do not receive financial aid to offset the cost of college. For those who do receive support, it typically only covers a modest portion of the cost. Students and their families still bear the brunt of the financial costs.

In the 2015–2016 school year, the average full-time-enrolled undergraduate student received a total of $9,740 in student aid ($8,390 in grants and $1,350 in tax credits and deductions). But a closer look between private and public school grants reveals a large funding gap. In the 2013–2014 school year, the average institutional grant for first-time, full-time undergraduate students at private schools totaled $13,840, while the average institutional grant for first-time, full-time undergraduate students at public schools was only $1,390.[7] When one revisits the annual cost of schooling, those grants still leave a large financial gap that has to be filled.

---

[7] Ma, Jennifer, Sandy Baum, Matea Pender, and Meredith Welch (2017), *Trends in College Pricing 2017*, New York: The College Board.

And, of course, not every student qualifies or receives institutional grants. In the 2013–2014 school year, merely 38 percent of first-time, full-time undergraduate students at public schools received a grant from their school, although 84 percent of first-time, full-time undergraduate students at private nonprofit schools received financial support from their school.

Even with the aforementioned institutional grants made directly from colleges, the bulk of costs still remains the responsibility of the student and their family. It should also be noted that most student grants are awarded on the basis of financial need. However, that often precludes upper-middle-class or upper-class families from qualifying for any meaningful offset to the cost of tuition.

The ever-increasing cost of college tuition, rising interest rates for student loans, the lengthening time for degree attainment, and the limited nature of college grants, combine to make 529 savings plans a remarkably useful tool with which grandparents can assist in their grandchildren's educational aspirations.

KEY CHAPTER TAKEAWAYS

- In all likelihood tuition will continue rising faster than inflation

- Students who borrow will be penalized with rising interest rates

- Most students take longer than four years to receive their degree

- Most grants are need based and only cover a fraction of total costs

Chapter 5

Is College Worth the Money?

In the face of ever-rising tuition expense and the media's portrayal of college graduates becoming minimum-wage baristas, is college still a good long-term investment for both students and parents? In a nutshell—yes! Looking at the financial return that a college degree generates over the course of one's working career, as well as the social returns over one's lifetime, it's evident that college is still an outstanding investment, albeit one that comes with a high price tag.

EARNINGS AND EDUCATION

In reality, it's difficult to find an objective analysis that doesn't demonstrate the long-term financial advantage of receiving a college degree. According to 2016 data the Bureau of Labor Statistics compiled, for persons aged twenty-five and above, median weekly earnings increase with each level of postsecondary education, while at the same time the rate of unemployment declines. Table 5.1 illustrates those findings.

Table 5.1

Earnings and unemployment by educational attainment in 2016[1]

Workers 25 years and older

EDUCATION LEVEL	MEDIAN WEEKLY WAGES	UNEMPLOYMENT RATE
No high school diploma	$504	7.4%
High school diploma	692	5.2%
Some college—no degree	756	4.4%
Associate's degree	819	3.6%
Bachelor's degree	1,156	2.7%
Master's degree	1,380	2.4%
Professional degree	1,745	1.6%
Doctorate degree	1,664	1.6%

One conclusion of a 2015 Georgetown University study is that over the course of a forty-year work career, a college degree holder will earn between $1 million and $3.4 million (depending on the field of study) more than an individual with a high school diploma.

When one looks at the unemployment rate for young workers between the ages of seventeen and twenty, the comparison is even more compelling. The Economic Policy Institute, using a twelve-month rolling average, examined the unemployment rate for this age group that was not enrolled in postsecondary schooling. In February 2016, they found that their unemployment rate was 17.9 percent, and that during the height of the 2008 recession in early 2010, the unemployment rate for nonschool-enrolled seventeen- to twenty-year-olds reached a staggering 28 percent! Regrettably, during difficult economic times, the less educated are the first to be laid off.[2]

[1] *Unemployment Rates and Earnings by Educational Attainment-2016* Washington DC: U.S. Bureau of Labor Statistics, Current Population Survey October 24, 2017.

[2] Kroeger, Theresa; Cooke, Tanyell; Gould, Elise; *The Class of 2016: The Labor*

You might be thinking, "I know college pays more years and years down the road, but what about those early years where a noncollegian is earning money and the collegian is shelling out for expensive tuition? Don't those initial years even things out?" No—and it's not even close.

An insightful comparison appears on the website *www.DegreeJungle.com*. According to their assessment that was published in 2017, during those initial four years, the average college graduate had spent $83,944 to attain their degree. However, during that same four-year time period, the high school graduate was earning an average total of $130,400. That's a $214,344 difference right off the bat. Yet because of the superior earning power, that $214,344 financial gap had been closed by the age of thirty, and after that point the degree holder's earning advantage began to snowball. DegreeJungle.com estimated that by the time both workers reached the age of sixty-five, the college graduate would have earned $820,000 more than his or her nondegree counterpart.

Inevitably, this raises the issue that college isn't right for everyone, which is a valid point. Many youth would be better served by receiving vocational training or earning an associate's degree in pursuit of the career they are most passionate about. And as grandparents, that's something you need to keep in mind. Not all your grandchildren will choose the same path in terms of what they want to do in life. One size doesn't fit all.

But My Grandchild Is a Genius and Doesn't Need College!

We all know individuals who have had exceedingly successful careers without attending college. If you're already a grandparent, you may

---

Market is Still Not Ideal for Young Graduates, Washington DC: Economic Policy Institute, April 21, 2016, *www.epi.org*.

have grown up in an area or era in which a formal education was simply less necessary than today.

I had an uncle who epitomized that era. Upon returning from the Pacific theater in World War II, Joel Pritchard worked at a small Seattle envelope manufacturer prior to successfully running for the state legislature. Later, he served for twelve years in the United States Congress, finishing his political career as Washington State's lieutenant governor. And while Joel Pritchard is probably better remembered for being a coinventor of pickleball, as opposed to spearheading environmental-related legislation, very few in or out of politics realized that Joel didn't have a college degree. And he could have attended college under the G.I. Bill.

That's a far cry from today when most serving in Congress have law degrees. But that was a different era. It was a period of less global competition, and there was less rapid technological change. It was an era that didn't automatically disqualify someone for not having a degree.

Yes, we can point to the likes of Bill Gates or Steve Jobs, who both dropped out of college and went on to revolutionize their industries and make billions in the process. If your grandchild is the next Bill Gates—congratulations! But such individuals are the extreme outliers, to say the least.

ALL COLLEGE DEGREES ARE NOT CREATED EQUAL

Ultimately, your grandchild's success depends on their underlying character: perseverance, intelligence, integrity, vision, optimism, ambition, and hard work. (All qualities I'm sure they've already inherited from their grandparents!) College helps focus and hone those traits toward achieving a specific career path.

The second biggest determinant in the financial value or return on a college investment is the major or field of study your grandchild chooses. The jokes about French poetry majors, from a strictly financial standpoint, often ring true. From the standpoint of marketability, and hence pay, all degrees are not created equal. The major your grandchild chooses usually has a significant impact on their future earnings and, as such, a huge impact on the financial return on their college investment.

One of the more compelling studies of different college majors' earning power is "The Economic Value of College Majors," conducted in 2015 by Georgetown University's Center on Education and the Workforce. The study highlights the average earning power of various fields of study over both the short and intermediate term. As one might expect, the Georgetown study found, on average, the "harder" subjects, such as those in the STEM categories (science, technology, engineering, and math) paid more handsomely than those that might be referred to as the "softer" studies, such as liberal arts. The chart below illustrates median annual wages in 2013 of college-educated workers (ages twenty-one to twenty-four) based on their majors.

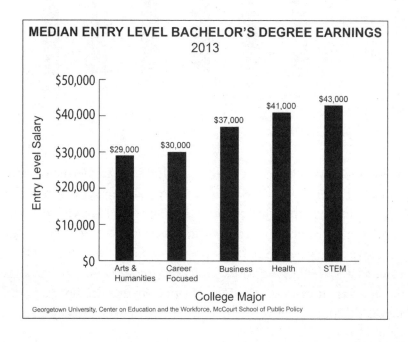

MEDIAN ENTRY LEVEL BACHELOR'S DEGREE EARNINGS
2013

Georgetown University, Center on Education and the Workforce, McCourt School of Public Policy

The Georgetown study also examined how various college majors faired at the midcareer level, which they defined as workers who were between the ages of twenty-five and fifty-nine. Here again, certain majors had earning advantages over others, and those advantages only grew over the course of time.

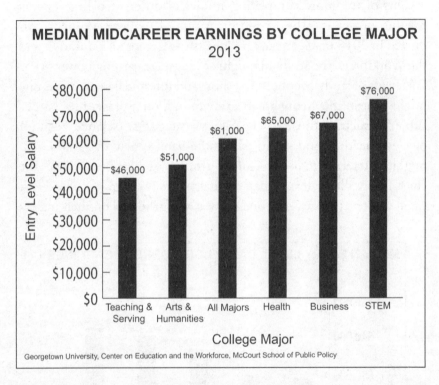

MEDIAN MIDCAREER EARNINGS BY COLLEGE MAJOR
2013

Georgetown University, Center on Education and the Workforce, McCourt School of Public Policy

The Georgetown University study concluded that the major your grandchild selects will have a bigger potential impact on their life-time earnings, or their long-term college financial return, than the underlying decision on whether or not to attend college. Over a for-ty-year working career, the study portrays whether to attend college or not as a $1 million decision. However, the variability of earnings among different majors is so wide, they portray that decision as a $3.4 million decision—between the highest and lowest earning majors.

However, it should be remembered that this, and other studies, use average earnings or median earnings. Individual results vary dependent on the individual traits mentioned earlier. There are liberal arts graduates earning far in excess of the averages, and STEM graduates earning far less. Majors are heavy influencers, but they are not destiny.

The financial and social benefits of a college degree are without question. College is most definitely still worth the price. And, depending on which school your grandchild finally attends, it may even give them a football, basketball, or hockey team to cheer for over the rest of their adult lives.

KEY CHAPTER TAKEAWAYS

- College is still a wise investment

- Degree holders typically far out-earn high school graduates

- International competition in a knowledge-based economy demands higher education

- Your grandchild's college major significantly impacts their career earnings

Chapter 6

INSULATING YOUR GRANDCHILDREN
FROM FINANCIAL ZOMBIES
(Student Loans)

Student loans are getting a lot of attention. Media pundits decry them as a house of cards which, like the subprime mortgage bubble and ensuing real estate crisis in 2008, could bring the U.S. economy to the brink of disaster. Granted, there is an enormous amount of student debt outstanding, and the growth rate of outstanding loans has accelerated. So, are student loans good or bad? Like any form of personal debt, student loans are a double-edged sword: They can be beneficial, or they can become a millstone around the neck of your loved ones. Grandparents have the potential to alleviate all or a significant portion of that financial burden.

This chapter will discuss the rising burden of student loans, why that growth has occurred, and its impact on individual borrowers and the economy at large.

Although the first U.S. student loans were offered in 1840 to Harvard University students, student loans weren't widely administered by the federal government until the passage of Title IV of the Higher Education Act of 1965. The government did subsidize the cost of college education for nearly half of our World War II veterans through the passage of the G.I. Bill in 1944. In the ensuing seventy-three years, nearly one-third of male veterans have used the G.I. Bill to attend college.[1]

For a student with no financial alternatives, or alternatives that don't fully cover the total cost of college, student loans can be a blessing. The ability to borrow funds at a favorable rate enables a student to attain the college education they couldn't otherwise afford. However, debt can also be a seemingly never-ending burden, akin to Sisyphus of Greek mythology, condemned for eternity with rolling a boulder uphill, only to watch it roll back down again just as he nears the top. This feeling can be particularly real for students who drop out of college or select an unmarketable major. In those difficult circumstances, debt creates a long-term financial burden for the student, adversely impacting their career, family, and housing decisions well into the future.

Trends in Student Loans

So, let's look at the facts. At the end of the first quarter of calendar 2018, there was a whopping $1.41 trillion in outstanding student loans owed by some 44 million Americans. The average monthly student loan payment was $351, while 10.7 percent of the outstanding loans were delinquent (ninety or more days in arrears or in actual default). To put that total debt into perspective, $1.41 trillion is $400 billion *more* than all outstanding U.S. credit card debt.[2] Why such staggering numbers? Simple—more and more students have had to borrow more and more money.

According to *Trends in Student Aid*, published by the College Board, total student loans taken out for the 1995–96 school year

[1] "State of Student Debt in the U.S. – Part 2", Center for Online Education, *www.onlinecolleges.net*

[2] "Household Debt and Credit Report, 1st Quarter 2018," Center for Microeconomic Data, New York: Federal Reserve Bank of New York, June 2018.

totaled $42.6 billion (in constant 2015 dollars). Annual borrowing peaked in 2010–11 at $124.2 billion, declining slightly to $106.8 billion in 2015–16. But since loans take ten or more years to repay, those steady annual increases have caused cumulative outstanding loans to balloon. Approximately 20 percent of U.S. households owe student loan debt, as does 40 percent of the population under the age of thirty-five, according to the Pew Research Center.[3]

By every measure, the student debt burden has been increasing right along with the rates of tuition increases. In 2016, the average student loan debt for a college graduate, encompassing both public and private colleges, who had borrowed for their schooling was $37,172, and 70 percent of all college graduates left school owing money.

But reserve your condolences for graduate students graduating with debt. While most media attention is focused on the cost of receiving a bachelor's degree, the cumulative individual debt held by students attending graduate school is dramatically higher. The graphic below, illustrates the average owed by individual students, as of 2012, who borrowed to attain their advanced degrees.

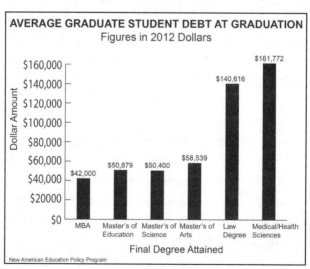

---

[3] DeSilver, Drew, "In Time for Graduation Season, a Look at Student Debt," Pew Research Center, FactTank – News in the Numbers, May 13, 2017, *www.pewresearch.org*.

The student debt burden even impacts older citizens. At the end of 2017, Americans aged 60 through 69 had six times more student debt, for either themselves or their children, than they did in 2004.[4]

So, why has aggregate student debt grown to such levels? First and foremost is the steady advance of tuition far and above the rate of inflation. Other factors include a surge of young adults returning to college amid the weak job market during the 2008 recession, a jump in attendance at nonselective, private for-profit schools, which over-promised graduate job opportunities, and even society's more relaxed attitude about debt. Regardless of where to point the finger, today's graduates have significantly more debt upon leaving school than any prior generation.

A GATHERING STORM?

On January 10, 2018, a prominent think tank alarmingly forecast that the student loan default rate for the graduating class of 2004 might very well reach 40 percent! A little over a week later, the United States Department of Education's Office of Inspector General reported that due to rising levels of indebted students taking advantage of income or wage-based debt repayment plans, federal student loans were in danger of becoming a net negative, or deficit, for the government.

Is the U.S. economy on the brink of an economic meltdown as wave after wave of student loan defaults bring down our financial system? No. Despite the rapid growth of student debt, the pace of which has actually abated of late, a doomsday scenario is highly unlikely. Whereas this is a troubling problem on a large scale, it is a very manageable problem. A number of factors limit the broad economic impact of student loan defaults.

---

[4] Gillers, Heather; Scism, Leslie; Tergesen, Anne; "A Generation of Americans is Entering Old Age the Least Prepared in Decades," The Wall Street Journal, June 22, 2018, *www.wsj.com*

Student loans versus home mortgages: The magnitude of student loans are dwarfed in comparison to home mortgages. A financial meltdown similar to the home mortgage and real estate collapse in 2008 is unlikely simply because the total value of student loans is small when compared to home mortgages. The dollar amount of total home mortgages is nearly six times larger than all outstanding student debt. And according to early-2018 data from the Federal Reserve, student debt represents less than 11 percent of all household debt in the United States. That's not to imply the rising debt isn't a concern, but it's not a concern likely to torpedo the economy.

Those who default on their loans: Look at who's actually defaulting on their student loans. While one out of every ten student loans is in default, which is a higher default rate than mortgages, car loans, or credit cards, the individuals defaulting on student loans are predominantly those owing the least amount of money. As of 2016, 66 percent of the borrowers in default owed $10,000 or less. Borrowers owing smaller amounts are typically students who, for whatever reason, have dropped out, deciding not to complete their degree requirements. Conversely, students owing the largest loan balances are typically graduate students with professional degrees, such as law or medicine. These students may finish schooling with extremely high debt levels of $150–200,000, but they are in career fields with compensation that can better support their high payments. The current default rate for debtors owing $40,000 or more is only 4 percent.[5]

The real impact to the overall economy in the rise of student debt, predominantly held by millennials, are the hidden costs associated with delayed consumption, delayed household formation (marriage), and delayed home purchase. As P.T. Barnum once said, "There is scarcely anything that drags a person down like debt."

---

[5] *Trends in Student Aid 2017*, The College Board.

Your Grandchildren's Debt Burden

Impact on economy: Millennials represent the United States' biggest demographic group and, as such, they are a major catalyst for our consumer-based economy. However, their debt weighs heavily on their wallets. According to Millennial Personal Finance's poll of millennial full-time workers with student debt, 46 percent would relinquish paid time off (PTO) from their employer in exchange for help with repayment.[6]

High levels of student debt dampen economic activity, either because monthly debt payments crowd out the capacity for major purchases, such as homes and autos, or because missed loan payments and outright default seriously damages a student's credit rating, thereby impeding their ability to borrow.

Home ownership - moving in with Mom and Dad?: Home acquisition by first-time buyers has long been a key driver of the economy. Beyond the house itself, home purchase triggers acquisition of durable goods, such as washers and dryers, not to mention the inevitable expenditures for home improvement and repair. However, in early-2017, the Federal Reserve Bank of New York reported a 35 percent decline in home ownership among millennials who were saddled with student debt. Not only does student debt repayment make monthly mortgage payments difficult, it can make saving enough for an initial down payment almost impossible. To no surprise, the Federal Reserve study found that the higher the level of student debt, the lower the level of home ownership when compared to those without student debt.

Declining entrepreneurship - a generation of cubicle dwellers?: In 2016, the Small Business Administration reported

---

[6] "What Do Young Workers Think About Student Loan Repayment Benefits?" Millennial Personal Finance, October 24, 2017, *https://bit.ly/2wvMN8m*.

that small business formation, entrepreneurship, was lower for current millennials than it had been for that age group in generations. Today's youth would seem to be more interested in working for someone than being self-employed. That's a troubling trend. Small businesses are the economy's engine, accounting for most of the jobs and new job creation in the United States. Many believe this is a direct result of millennials' high student debt burden, which coerces them toward a stable and consistent paycheck with which to service their loans. This apparent aversion to the financial uncertainty of starting a business may be the most insidious impact of student debt; it is smothering millennials' initiative.

DISCRETIONARY INCOME: Although not as economically impactful as deferring a home purchase, high debt payments also equate to less funds available for clothes, vacations, dining out, and other discretionary expenses.

DEBT PAYMENTS NOT QUALIFIED EXPENSES: Enterprising grandparents might wonder if student loan payments are considered qualified higher education expenses and thus payable from a 529 plan. Unfortunately not. Distributions from 529 savings plans used to assist your grandchildren with student loan repayment would be subject to income tax and the 10% penalty on the earnings portion of the withdrawn amount.[7]

THE LONG SHADOW OF DEFAULT OR ZOMBIE LOANS

When a borrower defaults on their student loan, it may adversely impact their credit rating for seven years, making it difficult, if not impossible, to obtain a car or home loan. Even if they can eventually attain

---

[7]   Schoenberger, Chana R., "College-Aid Offers Aren't Set in Stone", Saving for College, *The Wall Street Journal,* April 9, 2018, *www.wsj.com.*

credit, the loan default, or the many missed payments appearing on their credit record, may force them to accept onerously high interest rates.

As of March 31, 2018, the number of individuals who hadn't made a payment on their student debt during the prior twelve months had climbed to 4.6 million persons. That's twice the number from only four years earlier, despite a growing economy and declining unemployment during the same period. When a borrower defaults, their debt doesn't disappear. Borrowers may ultimately have their wages garnished.

While nearly every other type of debt can be eliminated through a bankruptcy filing, that's not the case with student loans. Hence, the financial zombies reference. They are the loans that cannot die. The widespread knowledge that it's nearly impossible to discharge student debt through bankruptcy is reflected in the fact that during 2017, out of the millions of individuals declaring personal bankruptcy, only 473 even bothered to request relief from their student loans.[8] However, as of mid-2018, that standard may be gradually changing.

Back in 1998, Congress eliminated the ability to discharge student loans in bankruptcy unless the borrower could prove "undue hardship." The financial rationale for this fell into the moral hazard camp. Lawmakers were concerned that opportunistic students would accumulate huge debts in attaining their degree or degrees and then simply declare bankruptcy, thereby eliminating their debts while walking away with their degree or degrees fully paid for by the taxpayers.

The current definition of undue hardship for the purpose of cancelling student debt dates back to the Marie Banner case of 1985. Ms. Banner attempted to cancel her student debt loans through personal bankruptcy. The presiding New York judge ruled that to do so, Banner had to prove undue hardship based on three criteria:[9]

---

[8] Ferek, Kathy Stech, "Judges Wouldn't Consider Forgiving Student Loans-Until Now," *The Wall Street Journal*, June 14, 2018, *www.wsj.com*.

[9] Friedman, Zack, "Can Student Loans Now Be Discharged in Bankruptcy?" *Forbes*,

a) the borrower has extenuating circumstances creating a severe financial hardship;

b) those circumstances are expected to continue for the term of the loan or the term of the repayment plan, which could last for twenty-five years; and

c) the borrower has made a good faith attempt to repay the loan.

As of this writing, many bankruptcy judges are attempting to find creative solutions to at least lessen the student loan burden if they're unable to discharge it in bankruptcy. Additionally, several members of Congress are formulating legislation that would provide a fairer litmus test for the undue hardship criteria. But for now, the financial zombie reference is all too accurate.

WHY HAVE STUDENT DELINQUENCIES RISEN?

In seeking the root cause for the miseries students burdened with large debt balances face, we return to the underlying rate of tuition inflation. Simply put, college tuition, and therefore student debt, has been rising at a faster rate than income. In some jobs there has been a real disconnect between the galloping rate of tuition increases and the tepid growth in the average wages of young borrowers. The following page illustrates the extent of the disconnect. Between 1992 and 2016 median household income grew from $51,390 to $59,039, a 15 percent increase. During that same period, the median debt load for graduating students grew from $17,500 to $37,172, an increase of 112 percent!

June 18, 2018, *www.forbes.com.*

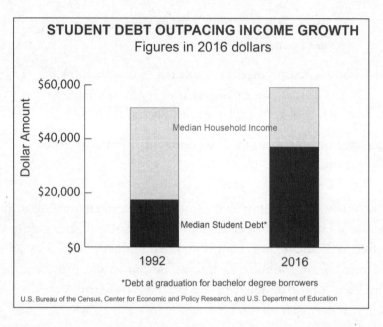

As previously discussed, despite rising tuition costs, a college degree, for the most part, will still provide a positive investment return over the course of your grandchild's earning career. Student loans, with government-subsidized interest rates and creative forms of repayment, offer one means of paying for some or all of that college degree. However, the debt burden can be very real. If grandparents are in the financial position to help relieve some of that potential student debt burden, that represents a lifetime gift for their eternally grateful grandchildren.

THE STUDENT LENDING LANDSCAPE

STAFFORD LOANS

Stafford Loans are made directly from the federal government to the borrowing student from the Federal Direct Student Loan Program (FDSLP). There are two types of Stafford Loans.

SUBSIDIZED STAFFORD LOANS: The loans account for 22 percent of all student loans made in 2015–16. Students receiving subsidized loans do not need to make loan payments until after graduation. Additionally, interest does not accrue on the loan while the student is in school. (Technically, the government pays the interest rate during this period.) As one might imagine, subsidized loans are targeted for students demonstrating financial hardship, often defined as a family with income below $50,000. A student's aggregate subsidized Stafford Loans cannot exceed $23,000 during their undergraduate years.

UNSUBSIDIZED STAFFORD LOANS: These loans account for 48 percent of all student loans made in 2015–16. If your grandchild has an unsubsidized loan, interest on the principal accrues during their time in school. Typically, loan and interest repayments are deferred until after graduation. Since these loans are not subsidized by the government, there is a much higher maximum for how much total debt a student may accumulate. In total, for both undergraduate and graduate studies, a student can amass as much as $138,500 in unsubsidized Stafford Loans. Medical students are afforded an even higher maximum. If your grandchild is pursuing a medical degree, they can borrow up to $40,500 per year and accumulate a total debt of $224,000 with this type of loan.

PLUS LOANS

Representing 19 percent of all student debt incurred in 2015–16, PLUS Loans are made to either the parents of undergraduate students, assuming those students are still considered dependents of their parents, or directly to the graduate student. Unlike Stafford Loans, there are no maximum borrowing limits, and they can be used to cover any education-related costs. PLUS Loans carry an interest rate higher than other federal-based educational loans.

Private Education Loans

Private education loans accounted for 10 percent of college-related loans made in 2015–16. Private loans originate from traditional commercial lenders, such as banks, and typically are made available for students or parents who still need additional funds for college after exhausting all other possible alternatives, such as grants, scholarships, and federal loans. In the case of federal loans, some families pursue private loans if they are financially overqualified for Stafford's need-based loans.

Perkins Loans

Perkins Loans represented a mere 1 percent of student loans in the 2015–16 school year. They have been reserved for students demonstrating severe financial hardship. In the past, they had a fixed interest rate of 5 percent, and interest did not accrue while the student was in school.

The Perkins Loan Program was effectively eliminated as of September 30, 2017. Although a helpful lending program for low-income families, Perkins Loans never accounted for more than 3–4 percent of any year's total student loans during the last twenty years.

Key Chapter Takeaways

- A combination of factors have generated an historic level of student debt

- Currently, the vast majority of student loans cannot be discharged in bankruptcy

- A student's debt burden will impact their family and housing decisions well into the future

Chapter 7

529 College Savings Plans Snapshot

The following provides a brief overview, or snapshot, of administrative and operational factors regarding 529 college savings plans. The nuts and bolts. More detailed information, with accompanying strategies specific to grandparents, follows in the remaining chapters.

Purpose

Conceptually, 529 college savings plans encourage families to save for postsecondary education by providing tax incentives. Specifically, funds set aside and invested for higher education can be later used for education-related expenses without incurring any federal taxes on the subsequent investment gains. At the end of 2017, college savings plans contained over $290 billion in assets.[1]

---

[1] Curley, Paul, "529 College Savings & ABLE, 529 Data Highlights: 4Q 2017," Strategic Insight, February 15, 2017, *www.sionline.com*.

ADMINISTRATION

STATE SPONSORSHIP: 529 plans are sponsored by individual states, and those states have significant latitude in setting the terms and conditions of their respective plans. Wyoming being the lone exception, each state and the District of Columbia has either a 529 savings plan, prepaid tuition plan, or both.

OPERATIONS: Most states outsource the day-to-day administration of their 529 plans to mutual fund companies, thereby benefitting from those organizations' economy of scale, technology platform, investment experience, and marketing expertise. For example, Fidelity Investments administers plans for Arizona, New Hampshire, and Delaware; T. Rowe Price oversees Alaska and Maryland; Vanguard manages Nevada; and TIAA-CREF administers nine state plans.

RESIDENCY REQUIREMENTS: A few states require that either the 529 plan account owner or the designated beneficiary be a state resident in order to utilize their sponsored plan. However, most states make their plans available for residents of any state.

DIRECT OR INDIRECT ACCESS: 529 accounts can either be accessed directly by the account owner in terms of establishing the plan, monitoring it, checking on investments, requesting distributions, and so forth, or can be accessed indirectly through a registered financial advisor. A few states offer only one manner of access while most offer both. Fees can vary significantly between the two methods of account access.

CREATING AN ACCOUNT: Establishing an account is straightforward, done either online or via hard copy forms.

OWNERSHIP AND BENEFICIARY

PLAN SETUP: Anyone can establish or contribute to a 529 savings plan on behalf of the designated beneficiary or future student. That includes friends, family members, particularly grandparents, or the beneficiary themselves. The account owner is the person who creates and oversees the savings plan. Additionally, 529 savings plans can be owned by legal entities, such as corporations, partnerships, or trusts.

CHANGING THE BENEFICIARY: The account owner can change the designated beneficiary for any reason without tax implications so long as the new beneficiary is a family relation to the original beneficiary. Qualified family members include the original beneficiary's:

- Spouse

- Son, daughter, or a descendant of the beneficiary's son or daughter

- Stepson or stepdaughter

- Brother, sister, stepbrother, or stepsister

- Father or mother, or ancestor of either parent

- Stepfather or stepmother

- Niece or nephew

- Aunt or uncle

- Spouse of any individual listed above, including the beneficiary's son-in-law, daughter-in-law, father-in-law, mother-in-law, brother-in-law, or sister-in-law

- First cousin

Common reasons to change the beneficiary might include the original beneficiary has dropped out of school, the original beneficiary has passed away or become disabled, or when the beneficiary has completed their education and there are funds remaining in the account.

ROLLING THE PLAN OVER: Funds from a 529 savings plans can be rolled over into a new or different 529 plan without adverse tax consequences, so long as funds are transferred within sixty days of distribution.

SUCCESSOR ACCOUNT OWNER: Upon establishing a 529 saving plan, the account owner will be asked to provide a successor account owner to oversee the account upon the death of the original owner. Should that occur, all the ownership rights and responsibilities pass to the successor.

TAXES

TAX-FREE GROWTH: While contributions to a 529 plan are made with after-tax dollars, all capital appreciation, dividends, and interest accruing in the account are free of federal taxation, so long as they are used for qualified postsecondary education expenses.

STATE INCOME TAXES: Most states with state income taxes provide additional incentives for 529 savers. Those incentives take the form of tax deductions or credits on state income taxes for 529 contributions or, in some cases, a partial matching of contributions.

GIFT TAX EXEMPTIONS: Contributors wishing to maximize the annual gift tax exemption can aggregate five years of the exemption into a single year. This is referred to as super funding the 529 plan. If the annual gift tax exemption amount was $15,000, an individual could contribute $75,000 into a 529 savings plan and the full amount would not count toward his or her lifetime maximum gifting allowance for tax purposes.

CONTRIBUTIONS

CASH ONLY: Contributions can only be made in cash (checks, money orders, cashier's checks, or credit card). In-kind contributions of stocks, bonds, mutual funds, or other securities are not permitted.

MAXIMUM CONTRIBUTIONS: Each state establishes a maximum dollar amount after which no additional contributions can be made to their respective 529 plan. Currently, account maximums range from a low of $235,000 to a high of $520,000. However, there are no limits on how large an account can appreciate.

CONTRIBUTIONS ARE NOT IRREVOCABLE: Funds contributed into a 529 savings plan can later be retrieved by the account owner. Some circumstances permit retrieval without tax consequences, such as the beneficiary receiving a scholarship. Otherwise, withdrawals for non-qualified expenses incur income taxes on the earnings portion of the distribution along with a 10 percent penalty on the earnings.

CREDITORS AND BANKRUPTCY

COLLATERAL: Assets held within a 529 savings plan cannot be pledged as collateral for a loan by the account owner.

PROTECTION FROM CREDITORS: Funds held in a 529 savings plan are protected from federal bankruptcy proceedings, so long as the designated beneficiary is the account owner's grandchild, child, stepchild, or stepgrandchild, including any of the foregoing through adoption or foster care, under the following guidelines:

- Funds are fully protected for any contributions made for the same beneficiary at least 720 days before bankruptcy filing.

- Funds contributed for the same beneficiary between 365 days and less than 720 days before bankruptcy filing are protected up to $6,225 (adjusted annually).

- Funds contributed into a 529 plan less than 365 days before bankruptcy filing are not protected in federal bankruptcy proceedings from creditors.

A number of states have additional safeguards and protections against creditors seizing 529 assets.

DISTRIBUTIONS

QUALIFIED EXPENSES: Distributions from a 529 savings plan incur no federal taxation on earnings, so long as funds are ultimately used for qualified educational expenses for the account's designated beneficiary at a qualified educational institution. Allowable expenses include tuition, mandatory fees, room and board, books, and computers. Qualified educational institutions are broadly defined to include everything from vocational trade schools to four-year private colleges to hundreds of international universities.

NONQUALIFIED EXPENSES: Distributions used for nonqualified purposes, or in excess of a given year's qualified educational expenses, are subject to tax on the earnings portion of the distribution payable at the account holder's marginal (highest) tax rate. Additionally, the

IRS imposes at 10 percent penalty on the earnings portion of the non-qualified distribution.

ANNUAL MATCHING: Withdrawals from 529 plans for specific educational expenses should be done in the same calendar year in which the expenses were incurred by the student or plan beneficiary.

IRS REPORTING: Any 529 plan withdrawals must be reported on IRS Form 1099-Q to demonstrate all funds were used for qualified educational expenditures. It is recommended that account owners retain copies of all education-related receipts in the unlikely event of an audit.

KINDERGARTEN THROUGH HIGH SCHOOL: While 529 plans were originally designed to only finance postsecondary education, as of January 1, 2018, up to $10,000 per year can be withdrawn for the beneficiary's private school tuition in grades K-12 without federal tax implications. (Depending on how recently said funds were contributed to the 529 account, there could be adverse tax implications at the state level if the state seeks to recapture previous state income tax deductions, credits, or matching funds.)

FINANCIAL AID

Grandchildren are not automatically disqualified from financial aid consideration because their grandparents have accumulated a 529 college savings plan on their behalf—even if that account has grown extremely large. Financial aid may be available from either the federal government or from the educational institution. In both cases, grandparent-owned 529 plans are not part of financial aid computations. However, once distributions are made, those monies weigh heavily against grandchildren and special care is necessary.

ESTATE ISSUES

REMOVED FROM ESTATE: Any contributions made to a 529 savings plan are removed from the contributor's estate, even though those monies can still be retrieved by the account owner.

INCOMPLETE SUPER FUNDING: If a contributor has super funded a 529 plan with five years of the annual gift-tax-exempt amounts into a single year and then passes away prior to conclusion of the five-year period, a prorated amount of the contributions is considered part of the estate for tax purposes.

INVESTMENTS

MULTIPLE INVESTMENT OPTIONS: There are three investment approaches available to 529 account owners, although not all states will offer all three:

- Individually created portfolio. Account owners can select from a menu of mutual funds, index funds, exchange-traded funds (ETF), and money market funds to create their own asset-allocated portfolio.

- Static portfolio. These are often referred to as target-objective portfolios. These are a preallocated combination of mutual funds, index funds, or ETFs with a specific objective, such as aggressive growth. The portfolio's objective never changes.

- Age-based portfolio. These are preallocated portfolios, but as the beneficiary approaches college age, the portfolios are rebalanced to become less volatile or risky. The purpose of the account becoming more conservative is to avoid a severe decline just as the student needs to access funds.

Changing investments: An account owner can change the investments in the account whenever the account's beneficiary is changed. If there is no beneficiary change, the investments can be changed two times per calendar year.

Investment fees: Investment fees vary significantly between state plans. Over an extended time period, seemingly minor fee differences have a significant impact on the final amount available for educational expenses.

Pooled investments: Account owner's funds are pooled with similar investors within the state plan, although each account owner receives a separate and individual account statement—just like mutual fund accounting.

The balance of this book covers the above in greater detail, as well as strategies and recommendations specifically suited for grandparents wishing to create or continue a family educational legacy for their grandchildren.

Key Chapter Takeaways

- Summary of 529 savings plan features and benefits:
    - Administration
    - Ownership and beneficiaries
    - Taxes
    - Contributions
    - Distributions
    - Financial Aid
    - Taxes
    - Estate issues

Chapter 8

MAXIMIZING TAX INCENTIVES

After building a significant 529 savings plan for the benefit of your grandchild, it may seem counterintuitive to suggest, or even insist, that their parents now pay thousands of dollars in tuition each year. However, there are a number of tax benefits your grandchild's parents can receive if they fund a portion of your grandchild's higher education costs, so long as they qualify. Those federal benefits may total as much as $2,500 per year. These additional federal tax benefits include The American Opportunity Credit, the Lifetime Learning Credit, and simply the ability to deduct qualified tuition payments from their taxable income.

A key consideration is that parents, or the students themselves, can only claim one type of educational tax credit or tax deduction each year. Additionally, educational funds withdrawn from a 529 savings plan will not qualify for any of the three federal tax incentives mentioned above. You've already received tax-free earnings on the 529 account holdings, and the federal government doesn't permit two tax incentives on the same dollars.

Let's examine the three tax incentives, how families might capitalize upon them, and the challenges in doing so.

THE AMERICAN OPPORTUNITY CREDIT

HOW IT WORKS: The American Opportunity Tax Credit (AOTC) provides a 100 percent tax credit on the first $2,000 of qualified educational expenses and a 25 percent tax credit on the next $2,000 of qualified educational expenses, for a total available federal credit of $2,500. Additionally, if the credit reduces your tax liability below zero, 40 percent of the unused tax credit, up to $1,000, is refundable to you, the taxpayer. IRS form 8863 is used to claim the credit.

WHO QUALIFIES FOR THE CREDIT: Here are the multiple requirements to claim the tax credit:

- Claimant must report the student as a dependent on their federal taxes. Most typically, this will be the student's parents. Grandparents are not excluded, so long as they're claiming the student as a dependent. To classify as a dependent, the child must be eighteen or younger at the end of the year or under twenty-four if a student.

- The AOTC is only available for the first four years of post-secondary education.

- The student must be enrolled at least half-time in a degree or certificate program.

- The claimant's tax filing status cannot be "married filing separately."

- The student cannot have a felony drug conviction as of the end of the tax year.

- The claimant's modified adjusted gross income (MAGI), which for most taxpayers is equivalent to their adjusted gross income (AGI), cannot exceed $90,000 for an individual or $180,000[1] for a couple filing taxes jointly.

- Qualified education expenses in this case do not include room and board.

The Lifetime Learning Credit

How it works: The Lifetime Learning Credit (LLC) provides a 20 percent tax credit on the first $10,000 of qualified education expenses for a maximum tax credit of $2,000. IRS form 8863 is used to claim the credit.

Who qualifies for the credit: Although a lesser credit than the AOTC, this has less stringent qualification criteria:

- Claimant must report the student as a dependent on their federal taxes. Most typically, this will be the student's parents. Grandparents are not excluded, so long as they're claiming the student as a dependent. To classify as a dependent, the child must be eighteen or younger at the end of the year or under twenty-four if a student.

- The LLC can be claimed for undergraduate, graduate studies, or improving job skills.

- Students do not need to be enrolled at least half-time and do not need to be enrolled in a degree or certification program.

- The claimant's tax filing status cannot be "married filing separately."

[1] These amounts for the 2017 tax year.

- The claimant's MAGI, which for most taxpayers is equivalent to their AGI, cannot exceed $66,000 for an individual or $132,000[2] for a couple filing taxes jointly.

- Qualified education expenses in this case do not include room and board.

TUITION AND FEES DEDUCTIONS

HOW IT WORKS: The third leg of the educational incentives triad are deductions up to $4,000 from taxable income for qualified education expenses. Actual savings depend upon the claimant's marginal tax bracket. Use IRS form 8917 to claim the deduction.

WHO QUALIFIES FOR THE DEDUCTION: This deduction is typically used by those who do not qualify for either the AOTC or LLC mentioned above.

- Claimant must report the student as a dependent on their federal taxes. Most typically, this will be the student's parents. Grandparents are not excluded, so long as they're claiming the student as a dependent. To classify as a dependent, the child must be eighteen or younger at the end of the year or under twenty-four if a student.

- No limit on the number of years the deduction can be made.

- The claimant's tax filing status cannot be "married filing separately."

- The claimant's MAGI, which for most taxpayers is equivalent to their AGI, cannot exceed $80,000 for an individual or $160,000[3] for a couple filing taxes jointly.

---

[2] Ibid

[3] Ibid

• Qualified education expenses in this case do not include room and board.

MAXIMIZING INCENTIVES

If your grandchild's parents qualify for either the AOTC, LLC, or the tuition expense deduction, it will be advantageous if they pay the first $4,000, or $10,000 in nonroom and board educational expenses, each year. This is the case even if you, the grandparent, have accumulated a large 529 plan that could easily pay all of your grandchild's postsecondary educational expenses. If parents qualify, making those initial tuition payments each year will generate tax credits totaling as much as $2,500.

If the situation warrants, grandparents might consider gifting or lending their grandchildren's parents sufficient funds so that they can make those initial tuition payments and thereby take advantage of the available tax benefits. Again, this can be done so long as the parents meet all qualification criteria. And remember, those funds cannot originate from the grandparent's 529 savings plan.

FLY IN THE OINTMENT?

In order to qualify for any of the three federal tax incentives previously described, the student must be a dependent of the person claiming the tax credit or deduction. The critical determinant in whether someone qualifies as a dependent is called the support test. Simply put, does the person claiming the education tax credit pay more than half of the student's living expenses? (Living expenses are defined to include food, shelter, clothing, medical and dental care, and education.)[4] If so, that student clearly qualifies as a dependent.

[4] Nichols, Nancy B.; Ferguson, Susan Q.; VanDenburgh, William M.; "Dependency Exemption Issues for College Students," The Tax Adviser, July 31, 2010, *www.thetaxadviser.com.*

However, the IRS has not specifically ruled one way or another on whether that student is still his or her parent's dependent if, while at school, their expenses are paid for with 529 plan distributions. A number of tax professionals contend that since 529 distributions sent directly to the school for room-qualified expenses are classified as student payments, and the student would appear on the 1099-Q educational expense form issued by the school, the student is supporting themselves. Accepting that perspective, the parents would no longer be able to claim the son or daughter as their dependent and, as such, could no longer claim any of the three federal educational tax incentives previously mentioned. The other side of the argument contends that since the 529 plan owner controls the account, can change the beneficiary, and even personally retrieve contributed funds, any 529 support for the student should be viewed as payment originating from the account owner, not the student. And as such, the student would still be the parents' dependent. (Assuming it's a parent-owned 529 plan.)

Grandparents or parents concerned with the apparent ambiguity in this area could take one of two conservative approaches if the parents are particularly keen to receive the available tax credits. One approach would be that the parents could personally pay at least 51 percent of their son's or daughter's total annual expenses, which would invariably include the first $4,000–$10,000 of tuition, thereby qualifying for whichever tax credit they are seeking. In light of the modest tax credit size compared to more than half of the student's total costs, this would seem to be a case of the tail wagging the dog.

A much more elaborate administrative exercise would entail the grandparents transferring a portion of their 529 plan to a parental 529 plan for the benefit of the same student. Funds could then be distributed directly to the parents, who in turn would reimburse the school for all qualified expenses. There would still be no taxes due on the earnings portion of the disbursements since they ultimately are used for qualified expenses. But the parents would have paid housing costs, and their names would appear on the 1099-Q form from the school.

Again, if parents qualify under all the other conditions, including not exceeding the MAGI, grandparents and parents are encouraged to discuss potential methodologies with their tax professional in order to claim any of the three federal tax incentives for qualified educational expenses.

KEY CHAPTER TAKEAWAY

- Grandparents should closely coordinate their grandchildren's college financing with parents for possible income tax credits and deductions

Chapter 9

FAMILY ISSUES

Imagine this scenario. It's your granddaughter's eighteenth birthday party—and it's a big affair. The entire family is present, including her other set of grandparents. At a lull in the festivities, you loudly clink your water glass to get everyone's attention. The room falls silent. All eyes are on you. You stand and loudly proclaim to all in attendance that, unbeknownst to your granddaughter, her siblings, her other grandparents, and even her parents, in your infinite wisdom and benevolence, you've decided that you're going to pay for all her college expenses. Broadly smiling, you sit down awaiting the family's adulation. What could possibly go wrong? Lots! Lots and lots could have gone wrong in that scenario.

COMMUNICATE RIGHT FROM THE START

At the earliest opportunity, perhaps even before the birth of your first grandchild, talk with your children about how meaningful it would be for you to financially assist with your grandchildren's educational costs. Sincerely explain why you'd like to take this step, what you're thinking of doing, and perhaps the dollar amount you hope to attain by the time your grandchildren are ready for college. I specifically said "thinking" of doing, since this conversation shouldn't be a one-way lecture. One of your children, or their spouse, may have particularly strong opinions that you'll need to take into consideration.

For example, what if your successful son-in-law or daughter-in-law often proclaims that they worked their way through community college, then went to a public in-state school without any help from anybody. It wasn't easy, but it built character. He or she believes that's why they've been successful in business. If that was good enough for him or her, it damn well will be good enough for their kids. He or she doesn't want their children to get so much as a nickel from anyone to help pay for their tuition or schooling. (A 2016 survey taken by Discover Financial Services found that 16 percent of parents believed children should be responsible for paying the full price of going to college.)[1]

Communicating as early as possible greatly reduces the chance of misunderstandings years later, allows time to resolve potential differences of opinion like the one cited above and, from a practical standpoint, enables parents to rethink their saving requirements. It might also open opportunities for specific colleges or universities that parents had previously assumed were out of reach. Even with an open communicative approach, there are still potential pitfalls.

BE MINDFUL OF OTHERS

It can be difficult to understand how your generosity could sow seeds of resentment or bitterness, but take a moment to view the world from their perspective. And while possible negative feelings may be more common with in-laws, don't neglect the feelings of your own children.

---

[1] "More Students Expected to Help Pay for College as Parents Become Less Worried about Costs," *Business Wire, Discover Student Loans*, May 9, 2016, *www.businesswire. com*.

YOUR CHILDREN AND THEIR SPOUSES: You wouldn't want financial support for your grandchild to appear as if you're trying to usurp parental authority and responsibility, or override the plans and dreams they envision for their children. And, of course, the financial aspect can weigh heavily on your children. Suppose your son-in-law is struggling in his career or has had difficulty holding down a job. Your unexpected largess could trigger feelings of inadequacy, resentment, and anger and could be interpreted as your trying to lord over them with your checkbook.

THE OTHER GRANDPARENTS: Your grandchildren's other set of grandparents may be unable to financially assist with their grandchildren's education. Regrettably, if those grandparents view gifts as some sort of competition (perhaps as a surrogate for their grandchildren's affections), your generosity can again generate feelings of inadequacy, anger, and ill will.

UNEVEN SUPPORT: There may be valid reasons for providing different levels of financial support to your different grandchildren. But be forewarned that those inequities will eventually be discovered, creating a family flash point, fomenting resentment among those grandchildren who feel unfairly shortchanged, and perhaps among their parents as well. Additionally, trumpeting your educational support family-wide may have repercussions with those who fall just outside your scope of generosity (e.g., great-nephews, great-nieces, cousins, etc.) Barring extreme situations, most family advisors recommend striving for equity in grandchildren's educational gifts.

Being mindful of how others could misinterpret your intentions, collaborating with parents, and being discreet in the specifics of your educational support will all go a long way in preventing potential family conflicts.

ATTACHING STRINGS

Should strings be attached to your 529 savings plan college gift? Should you compile a list of things your grandchild must do or mustn't do to qualify for your eventual financial support? At the end of the day, it's your money. Since you can always retrieve funds deposited into a 529 plan, creating requirements is certainly a possibility. But give it serious consideration before drawing lines in the sand.

Many parents attach requirements to pay for all or a portion their children's college tuition. These can run the gamut from a gentle nudge to rigid dictates. Some of the more common strings I've heard from parents have included:

- "I'll pay for your schooling but only if you attend my alma mater (or join my fraternity/sorority)."

- "We'll pay the cost of a public college, but if you want to attend private school, you'll have to make up the difference yourself."

- "We'll pay tuition if you pick a sensible major that will lead to a sensible job. If you want to major in something like art, you're on your own."

- "We'll pay some of it so long as you work a part-time job while you're in school."

- "We'll only pay for in-state tuition!"

- "I'll pay for your school so long as you maintain a 3.0 grade point average."

- "We'll pay for four years of schooling. If it takes you longer or you want to go to graduate school, you'll have to pay for that."

One or two reasonable strings attached to college funding isn't such a bad thing. But if the strings you attach to tuition are onerous and obtrusive, your gift may be viewed as a cudgel with which to control your grandchildren's lives, something that won't be appreciated by your grandchildren or their parents. Sadly, that could turn a transformational gift for which your grandchildren are eternally grateful into a point of frustration and resentment, despite the gift's generous size.

Whether behavioral strings should be attached to your grandchildren's tuition misses the most important question: Are grandparents really the ones who should be determining those criteria? You're not the parents. And perhaps that's the most important takeaway of this discussion. If grandparents create demanding preconditions to release funds from their 529 plans, even with the best of intentions, they begin to slip into the role of parenting. They will unwittingly enter the no-win minefield of who should be performing that role. Whether you like it or not, unless the parental situation is extreme—substance abuse, neglect, incarceration—it's the parents who call the shots about raising your grandchildren, just like it was when you raised your children.

I recommend grandparents cut the strings. Don't inadvertently attempt to control or dictate your grandchildren's education. If you have specific hopes or concerns, share them with their parents, but do so as a caring and thoughtful grandparent as opposed to a dominating family tyrant. Yes, your grandchildren will inevitably make a mistake or two in pursuit of their higher education objectives. But remember, you're not their parents, so fight the urge to be overly protective and rigid. Nudge, don't push. Grandparents make wonderful coaches but poor bosses. And that leads to one parting observation.

MANAGE YOUR EXPECTATIONS

After nearly two decades of wistfully watching your grandchildren mature into young adults, and your 529 savings plans steadily appreciate, it's natural to hold out the highest of hopes. Because of your foresight, encouragement, and support, your grandchild now has the opportunity to achieve their potential and pursue their dreams at some of the finest learning institutions in the world. You've visualized them at Harvard Law School, studying medicine at Johns Hopkins, music at Juilliard, or perhaps graduating from Stanford's Graduate School of Business. But that may not be the case.

If you've personally sacrificed, perhaps more than anyone knows, to help provide for your grandchild's or grandchildren's higher education, it can be disappointing and disillusioning to see them chart an educational course that appears extremely suboptimal. It's helpful to remember the advice you undoubtedly embraced when your own children were young:

Not everyone takes the same path—even if they're traveling towards the same destination.

If your grandchildren select a path wildly different from the path you took, the path their parents took, or the path you believe they should take, be gracious. It is their life after all, and the decisions they make in the first year or two at college won't permanently cast their futures. Generally, it's almost the opposite. So long as your grandchildren are learning and responsibly moving ahead in their journey toward adulthood, then they're using your gift well.

At the end of the day, parents and grandparents want the same thing for their children or grandchildren: for them to lead happy and productive lives. Education can play an important role in accomplishing that. But because money and family can be a volatile combination, it would serve grandparents well to be mindful of the potential points of friction and act accordingly.

Key Chapter Takeaways

- Grandparents should communicate with their grandchildren's parents as early as possible about their plans for financial assistance

- Grandparents should be aware of how their generosity could be misunderstood by other family members

- Exercise caution in attaching strings to your gift

- Respect your grandchild's educational decisions

Chapter 10

CONTRIBUTION STRATEGIES

There are so many potential variables involved in funding optimization of your grandchildren's 529 savings plans, it would be extremely easy to overcomplicate the process. This chapter will attempt to address a few key contribution strategies to assist grandparents in maximizing the utilization of their 529 plans. Contribution considerations include the availability of funds, your income tax bracket, your home state's income tax 529 deductibility, the size of your estate, and whether you foresee withdrawing funds for K-12 private school tuition (now a possibility under the Tax Cuts and Jobs Act of 2017). Despite the factors above, for the overwhelming majority of grandparents the best 529 contribution timing strategy is also the simplest:

Contribute as much as you can as early as you can

That's all there is to it. Pretty simple. Why? Because the financial power of long-term, tax-free compounding, combined with reasonable investment returns, far outweighs the modest benefits of a state income tax deduction.

Let's look at the numbers. Consider a retired couple, financially fortunate enough that they can make a large lump-sum contribution into a 529 savings plan upon the birth of their granddaughter. They establish a 529 savings plan with a deposit of $200,000, an amount roughly equal to three years at a private Ivy League university. (Remember, the couple can always access those funds if necessary.) If we assume the account appreciates tax-free at an average annual compounded rate of 7 percent, on their granddaughter's eighteenth birthday, her 529 savings plan will have grown to $675,986. Not too bad.

Now suppose that same couple lives in New York, a state with higher-than-average state income tax rates, but one that rewards 529 contributors with an annual dollar-for-dollar tax deduction up to $10,000. The couple's marginal state income tax rate is 6 percent. Instead of contributing that same $200,000, at their granddaughter's birth, they've decided to establish a 529 savings plan with an initial contribution of $20,000; for the next eighteen years on their granddaughter's birthday, they'll contribute $10,000 to take advantage of New York's state tax deduction. (Like most states, New York doesn't permit contributions in excess of the annual $10,000 to be carried over to the following year.) And they're even going to take the amount they saved in state taxes each year and add that amount to their annual $10,000 529 contribution. They're still contributing a total of $200,000, plus the tax savings. Pretty clever. How'd they do? For all their long-term planning, not as well. Under this scenario, on their granddaughter's eighteenth birthday and after their final contribution, they've only amassed $417,388. That's a whopping 38 percent reduction in available funds!

How can that be? By needlessly stretching out their contributions, they've lost the tax-free investment growth on the bulk of their funds in the earlier years—all for a modest annual tax savings of $600 ($10,000 deduction at their 6 percent tax rate). It usually doesn't pay to chase after state income tax deductions at the expense of a longer investment time horizon.

Now, to be fair, we all know financial markets do not increase in a lockstep consistent fashion year in and year out. Real-world volatility (up one year and down the next) can dramatically impact long-term returns just from a single down year, which is what makes dollar cost averaging an advantageous funding process for many investment vehicles.

Using a real-world comparison assumes that our New York-based couple's granddaughter was born on January 1, 1999, and at that time, they either started a 529 plan with $200,000, or started the plan with $20,000 and made eighteen subsequent additions of $10,000 plus their annual state income tax savings. Using annual returns for the S&P 500 Index, this period includes what investment professionals call The Lost Decade, straddled by the Dotcom Crash, and the 54 percent market decline during the 2008–2009 Great Recession. We even excluded the bullish investment returns of 2017. That represents a very difficult eighteen years in the markets. Results? Still not very close.

On their granddaughter's eighteenth birthday, the staggered contribution strategy would have grown to $438,088. But by adhering to the strategy of donating as much as you can as early as you can, the initial $200,000 contribution would have grown to $511,992, a 17 percent increase in available college funds. Over an extended time period, in this case eighteen years, it's hard to overstate the advantage of tax-free compounding.

While the majority of states with state income tax deductions or credits for 529 contributions do not permit carrying forward excess contributions (deductions) into the next year, there are a few states that do. For example, state residents establishing 529 plans in Ohio, Louisiana, Rhode Island, Virginia, and Wisconsin have no limit on the number of years they can carry forward any excess contributions above the annual limit. Residents of these states can receive ongoing annual tax deductions even when making a large one-time gift. A few other states (Arkansas, Connecticut, Maryland, Oklahoma, Oregon, and Illinois) have a limit on how long the excess tax deduction can be carried forward. For example, Illinois permits a five-year carryforward. Residents of these states really can have their cake (long-term, tax-free compounding) and eat it too (state income tax deductions).

WHAT ABOUT GIFT TAXES?

Prior to passage of the Tax Cuts and Jobs Act of 2017, financial planners and other proponents of 529 savings plans encouraged their clients to focus on the annual gift tax exemption, whereby a single grandparent in 2018 could give up to $15,000 to as many persons as they wanted without any gift tax consequences. A married couple could make a $30,000 gift to as many persons as they wanted without incurring any tax consequences. Additionally, 529 regulations permit combining five years of maximum tax-excluded gifts, totaling either $75,000, or $150,000, into a single year; the process can be repeated again in another five years, and so on. The industry calls this super funding.

That makes for very generous 529 contributions. For example, if our two grandparents living in New York had six grandchildren, and had the available funds and the desire to do so, they could contribute $150,000 into a 529 plan for each grandchild for a total of $900,000 in a single year without any adverse gift tax implications.[1] The gift tax exclusion also applies to the generation-skipping tax (GST) in which, as the name implies, the IRS taxes large gifts that skip over one family generation to the next. Since gift taxes and generation-skipping taxes start at 40 percent, this approach attracted a lot of attention.

However, with the passage of the Tax Cuts and Jobs Act of 2017, an individual's lifetime exclusion for total cumulative gifts was doubled from $5.6 million to $11.2 million. For a married couple, that

---

[1] They would need to complete IRS Tax Form 709 to report the aggregation of their gifts.

lifetime exclusion totals a sizeable $22.4 million. That figure incorporates all gifts made during your lifetime, or even after, passed through your estate. That sets a pretty high hurdle for when single grandparents or a married couple need to worry about gift taxes. Most couples' lifetime giving and estates are well, well below that $22 million figure. Estimates from the Joint Committee on Taxation and Tax Policy Center indicate that those large estates will only represent 0.07 percent of all estates settled in 2018, or about one out of every 1,430 estates.[2]

This means that the overwhelming majority of grandparents wishing to fund 529 college savings plans for their grandchildren can ignore any potential tax ramifications of their gifts and instead focus their giving based on more relevant factors, such as individual grandchildren, multigenerational educational goals, and maximizing tax-free investment returns.

It should be noted that contributing to a 529 plan above the current annual exemption amount of either $15,000 or $30,000 still necessitates that you or your tax preparer complete IRS Form 709, the United States Gift (and Generation-Skipping) Tax Return.

IF YOUR ESTATE EXCEEDS $11.2 OR $22.4 MILLION

There are exceptions to every guideline. If you're in the fortunate financial position whereby large contributions to a grandchild's 529 plan will trigger federal gift and/or estate taxation, then a different contribution strategy is warranted. Gift taxes in excess of your lifetime exemption quickly ramp up to the maximum 40 percent rate. Even taking into account tax-free compounding, that tax rate creates an extremely high hurdle rate to overcome.[3]

---

[2] To illustrate how restrictive gift and estate taxes used to be, back in 1980 when this author began work in the investment field, the gift and estate tax exemption was only $161,000, and the top estate and gift tax rate was a staggering 70 percent. That's a far cry from today's $22 million lifetime exemption.

[3] In running numerous scenarios, both at static annual rates of return and the actual

Grandparents in this situation should seriously consider a super funding approach when establishing a grandchild's 529 savings plan. Grandparents utilizing this tactic would contribute their combined maximum annual gift tax exemption amount of $30,000 in Year #1—preferably late in the calendar year. Then, in the beginning of calendar Year #2, they would contribute five years of annual gift tax exemptions compressed into that single year, totaling another $150,000 contribution. Permitted under IRS regulations, this contribution represents the annual gift-exempt amount for Years #2 through #6.

If the $30,000 gift is made towards the end of Year #1 and the $150,000 gift is made toward the beginning of calendar Year #2, the couple has contributed a total of $180,000 in the space of less than a year. This could literally be accomplished in the span of a few weeks if done during the last and first days of the Years #1 and #2 respectively. And all done with no gift tax consequences.

After Year #6, a couple could contribute another $150,000 at the start of Year #7 if they wished to do so, and those new monies would represent five years of annual gift tax exemptions for Years #7 through #11. In this example, grandparents have contributed a total of $330,000 in just over a six-year period and have avoided a 40 percent tax on their gifts. (They could do the same once again in Year #12.) And use of the annual gift tax exemption, even when compressed into five-year blocks, can be used for an unlimited number of grandchildren, great-nieces and nephews, or any family members.

Contributing the Maximum Allowable Amount

If you have both the desire and the financial resources to create the largest education fund possible for each of your grandchildren,

returns from several state plans between 2000–2017, avoiding the 40 percent gift tax more than compensates for the reduction in funds immediately available for tax-free compounding.

perhaps with the intent of excess funds being used for your eventual great-grandchildren's education, the state in which you establish your 529 plans is of paramount importance.

The underlying purpose in the legislative creation of 529 savings plans was to help finance a postsecondary education and, as of 2018, those same funds can also be used for K-12 private school tuition up to $10,000 per year. Since college savings plans were never intended to simply become an unlimited tax-free investment account, there are restrictions on how much can be contributed. Specifically, contributions can no longer be accepted into a 529 savings plan once the balance exceeds the anticipated costs of your grandchild's qualified higher education costs. However, that's a pretty ambiguous guideline.

Each individual state has wide latitude in how they define qualified costs of education. Originally, most states adopted the federal safe harbor guidelines of five years of tuition, fees, textbooks, and room and board for the most expensive college or university within the 529 plan universe. Lately, more and more states have leniently redefined their guidelines to not only include the costliest undergraduate schools in the United States, but to include the costs required to attend the costliest graduate schools as well. And most states increase those limits every few years to accommodate the rising cost of tuition.

As one might expect, despite the more flexible criteria, individual states vary significantly on what they define as the maximum amount required to fund a beneficiary's education. During 2017, that figure ranged from a low of $235,000 in Georgia and Mississippi to a high of $520,000 in New York. If your primary goal is to maximize funding, then selecting a state with a high maximum contribution will obviously be a key factor when establishing your 529 plan.

State contribution maximums are per beneficiary (grandchild), not per 529 savings plan. So, if both you and your grandchild's parents create a 529 savings plan in the same state, the state combines the amount in those two plans to determine whether the maximum amount has been reached.

For grandparents wishing to maximize their 529 plan gifting for the added purpose of removing those assets from their taxable estate (covered in more detail in Chapter 19) and who plan to fund the accounts over time in accordance with the annual gift tax exemption limits, there is a potential trap to avoid. Once a 529 savings plan reaches the state's maximum contribution level, you are unable to make any more contributions, regardless of how the account reached that level.

For an extreme example, suppose two grandparents living in Biloxi, Mississippi, wish to establish a 529 plan for their grandson and want to contribute the maximum allowable in the state—$235,000. Being mindful of gift taxes, they superfund the account contributing $180,000 over a two-month period that straddles two calendar years. (This represents the $30,000, maximum for the first year with the $150,000 balance representing five years of compressed contributions for years two through six.) A little over five years later, these same grandparents want to contribute the remaining $55,000 to reach the $235,000 maximum contribution level. But wait! In the intervening time period, the account has appreciated and is now valued at $250,000. That's a solid return, but now the account's value exceeds the maximum contribution. The grandparents cannot contribute any more unless the account declines back under the $235,000 level. In a way, this is a good problem to have since the account is successfully appreciating. But for grandparents who hope to remove more assets from their estate, or simply maximize the plan's balance, this could be a frustrating situation.

HOW CAN I CONTRIBUTE WHEN I DON'T EVEN KNOW HOW MANY GRANDCHILDREN I'LL HAVE?

One of the lesser-known, but more valuable, 529 characteristic is the plan-to-plan transfer flexibility. Funds can be completely or partially transferred from one 529 savings plan to another.

Consider the hypothetical plight of brand new grandparents who wish to begin a family educational legacy. Our new grandparents have six children, the oldest of which just delivered their first grandchild. Hooray! Now they'd like to fund a 529 savings plan as generously as possible. But if they're blessed with a dozen or more grandchildren, and they fund the early grandchildren's plans too generously, they might not have enough left over for the tenth, eleventh, or twelfth grandchild. Should they just wait until all their children have finished having grandchildren before they start creating 529 plans?

Absolutely not! The ability to transfer money between 529 plans enables them to establish the first educational fund with a significant amount, perhaps their state's maximum, and then transfer a portion of it to future 529 plans for additional grandchildren—and augmenting those future funds with new money as necessary. This enables our new grandparents to take advantage of long-term, tax-free investment appreciation as early as possible, while finalizing the allocation per grandchild later. And if they end up having those twelve grandchildren— congratulations!

Specifics vary from state to state, but transfers or partial rollovers occur with no tax consequences, so long as the transfers occur between family members. Family members are defined by the relationship with the 529 beneficiary (grandchild) and include siblings, stepsiblings, parents, stepparents, aunts, and uncles. (See Chapter 7.) Assuming your grandchild is married prior to completing their higher education, transferable family members also include your grandchild's children, stepchildren, nieces, nephews, father-in-law, mother-in-law, spouse, first cousins, or the spouse of any of the above. That's a lot of flexibility!

In most state plans, when making a fund transfer, you can select from which investments the money is withdrawn and into which investments the money should be allocated in the receiving 529 plan. That's an important element since grandchildren of different ages will normally need different investment allocations. The majority of state plans do not have limitations on how many times per year transfers can be made, which is good in case those six hypothetical children all add to their families at the same time.

529 plan transferability also gives grandparents the ability to fine-tune their educational funding. How to fairly juggle the inevitable disparity in education is a personal grandparent decision. This situation arises when one grandchild will be attending Harvard Law School and another a local community college. The ability to transfer funds between 529 plans without consequence provides grandparents the opportunity to individually customize their financial support of each grandchild.

KEY CHAPTER TAKEAWAYS

- Contribute as much as you can as early as you can

- Utilize super funding if gift taxes are a concern

- Don't by overly influenced by modest state income tax deductions

Chapter 11

INVESTING 529 PLAN ASSETS

After generously establishing a 529 plan for one or more of your grandchildren, and drawing upon your own hard-earned savings to do so, the last thing you want is poor investment performance. Lackluster returns dilute the benefit of long-term, tax-free compounding, which is the whole point of funding a 529 plan as early and as generously as possible.

When Benjamin Franklin passed away in 1790, the terms of his will left $4,500 to the city of Boston for philanthropic purposes. But there was a catch! The city couldn't access the funds for one hundred years. Franklin wanted his bequest to benefit from investment compounding so he could provide Boston with a more meaningful gift. One hundred years later in 1890, Franklin's gift had grown to nearly $400,000, almost ninety times its original amount, which would be worth over $10 million in today's dollars. Tax-free compounding is without question the greatest advantage of 529 college savings plans. Albert Einstein called compound interest, "the greatest mathematical discovery of all time."

529 Qualified Tuition Plans

As mentioned earlier, there are two types of 529 qualified tuition plans with very different underlying investment approaches.

Prepaid tuition plans: As the name implies, prepaid tuition plans enable an account owner to purchase college credits or units at participating colleges and universities at today's prices for tomorrow's tuition. Typically, these cover in-state public university tuition, while excluding room and board. From an investment standpoint, prepaid tuition plans are similar to an old-fashioned pension retirement plan. As a retiree, you've been guaranteed a certain level of retirement income, or a defined benefit. It's up to your former employer to make those payments and to make prudent investment decisions to ensure those payments continue. Although you're a beneficiary of the pension plan, you have no responsibility or input on how those funds are invested.

In the case of a prepaid tuition plan, the state in which your plan is based invests the proceeds of your credit or unit purchases in the expectation that their investment returns will offset the difference between today's tuition price and tomorrow's.

College savings plan: The 529 college savings plans, with respect to investments, more closely resemble 401(k) retirement plans. The employee determines how much they want to invest and how those funds are to be invested from a menu of investment options their employer provides. Unlike the pension plan analogy cited above, there are no retirement income guarantees. Your retirement income is determined by how much you elect to contribute, how you choose to invest those monies and, of course, the performance in the financial markets during those intervening years. A 529 savings plan works in the same manner.

In order for a 529 savings plan to meet the Internal Revenue Service's regulatory requirements, it must enable the account holder (grandparents) or even the account beneficiary (grandchild) the ability to either directly or indirectly guide the investments of any contributions made to the plan. The IRS permits you to change your investments whenever you change the beneficiary designation of the plan, for example, switching from one grandchild to another. However, since the plans were never intended to accommodate market timing or day trading, aside from the changed beneficiary situation, plan investments cannot be changed more than two times per calendar year.

You're Not Investing for Retirement

While there are investment similarities between a 529 savings plan and a 401(k) retirement plan, there is a critically important distinction between the two: time. With a college savings plan, you typically have an eighteen-year period of accumulation, while you can have thirty to forty years to build retirement assets. Additionally, those college funds may only be used over a four- to six-year period, while retirement funds may need to last thirty or more years. This difference has significance in how funds are invested.

Upon a grandparent's retirement, most financial professionals would recommend he or she retain a portion of their portfolio in equities (stocks) to provide potential growth to help offset inflation. It wouldn't be prudent to place 100 percent of a retiree's holdings into fixed income (bonds), particularly at the time of this writing when interest rates sit near historic lows. Additionally, due to the thirty-year retirement horizon, advisors generally recommend only withdrawing 4 percent per year to ensure funds will last over the coming three decades. That long-term planning horizon, coupled with a modest withdrawal rate, would enable an investment portfolio to successfully weather the occasional bear market one could expect along the way.

But college is different. Your grandchildren's college expenses will be compressed into a four- to six-year window, which will necessitate a very high withdrawal rate from your 529 plan. That creates significant risk for your grandchild's education if the financial markets experience a major decline just as your grandchild begins college. Your 529 savings plan no longer has the time to earn back those lost dollars and you'd be forced to liquidate securities at a loss. These characteristics, unique to financing a college education, are the key components in selecting among the three 529 investment methods.

529 Savings Plan Investment Options

The vast majority of 529 savings plans require the account owner to select an investment portfolio that contains mutual funds, exchange-traded funds (ETFs)[1], or certificates of deposit that the state 529 plan administrator has provided. There are three distinct investment approaches, the third of which is recommended and by far the most widely utilized.

An individually created portfolio: This approach enables the account owner to create their own 529 portfolio from a menu of individual investments available in the plan. Independent investment options are primarily mutual funds and ETFs. The resulting portfolio can be as aggressive or conservative as the account owner desires. This approach would only be recommended for a grandparent or grandparents who possess the requisite investment expertise, knowledge, time, and temperament to not only create the original portfolio but to monitor and rebalance it as necessary in the ensuing years.

Target-objective or target-risk portfolios (static portfolios): Static portfolios provide the account owner with a pre-allocated collection of mutual funds and ETFs designed to attain specific investment objectives with a level of acceptable risk. Static portfolios

---

[1] An ETF, or an exchange traded fund, is a security that tracks an index or a basket of assets like an index fund with greater liquidity and lower fees than mutual funds.

have names such as "growth and income," "principle preservation," or "aggressive growth." These portfolios provide diversification of assets, but they are most heavily weighted in line with their stated objectives. For example, an aggressive growth portfolio would predominately contain equities, including domestic, international, and emerging markets, but it would also hold a small percentage of bonds.

These pre-allocated portfolios are designed to be as efficient as possible, providing the best possible return for the acceptable level of risk, or the least risk for the intended return objective. Additionally, the plan administrator will rebalance these portfolios on a quarterly or annual basis to ensure they retain their intended composition. This is typical portfolio construction in line with modern portfolio theory.[2]

However, the disadvantage lies in why these portfolios are called static, despite the occasional rebalancing. This portfolio's long-term allocation never strays significantly from the primary objective, such as aggressive growth. But as your grandchild nears college enrollment and needs access to those funds, an aggressive and highly volatile portfolio that was appropriate when he or she was in kindergarten simply isn't any longer. A severe and prolonged market correction just before they need funds to pay their freshman tuition might put a real crimp in their plans. Therein lies the major advantage of the third and final investment option available in 529 plans.

AGE-BASED PORTFOLIOS: An age-based investment approach is similar to target-date retirement options available in most 401(k) retirement plans. The typical asset structure starts with a heavy allocation of equities so as to maximize potential growth opportunity during your grandchild's early years. That also provides ample time to recoup any short-term losses as the market fluctuates. Then, as your grandchild ages, the 529 plan administrators reduce the stock exposure, adding more and more bonds to the mix. In that manner, the portfolio

---

[2] Modern portfolio theory (MPT) is a theory in which portfolios are constructed with different asset classes with a mathematical framework to minimize risk.

becomes more insulated against significant losses at the time when your grandchild will need that money for tuition. As Ron Popeil[3] would have said, this is a "Set it, and forget it" approach.

The reallocation of holdings is accomplished in one of two ways: reducing the stock holdings within the actual portfolio or moving all the funds into a different, more conservative portfolio.

AGE-BASED PORTFOLIOS

While this is essentially a hands-off method for the 529 account owner, there are four factors you'll want to consider prior to making your investment decision:

RISK PROFILES AND GLIDE PATHS: Most 529 state-sponsored, age-based investment programs offer three different risk-related tracks from which to choose: aggressive, moderate, or conservative. If the funds will be invested in the 529 plan for ten or more years, this single choice will have the greatest impact on your investment returns. While all three of these investment tracks will gradually hold fewer stocks and more bonds, an aggressive program will do so with a higher allocation of equities throughout the life of the program than the moderate or conservative track. Conversely, the conservative track will hold more fixed income investments than the aggressive or moderate allocations at comparable points in time.

Chart 11.1 displays the percentage of stock holding in Iowa's aggressive growth track, Kansas's moderate track, and Pennsylvania's conservative investment track based on the age of the account's beneficiary. The lower the stock component in a portfolio, the less risky, or less volatile, it becomes and typically with less return. This downward-sloping reduction in stock holdings is referred to as the 529 portfolio's glide path.

---

[3] Ronald M. "Ron" Popeil is an inventor and promotional personality, best known for his direct marketing company Ronco.

Chart 11.1

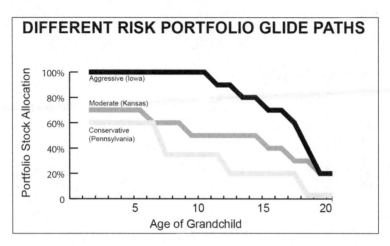

DIFFERENT RISK PORTFOLIO GLIDE PATHS

In the three portfolios illustrated, the aggressive option begins with a 100 percent commitment to stock, with the moderate holding 70 percent, and the conservative only 60 percent. By the time the beneficiary reaches the age of seventeen and is close to college age, the conservative portfolio holds no stock, the moderate holds 30 percent, and the aggressive portfolio still has 40 percent invested in equities.

Perhaps surprisingly, despite the same risk profile label, the stock-to-bond holdings within these age-based portfolios can vary significantly between states. All aggressive-growth, age-based investment tracks, for example, are not created equal. While most states' investment options are turnkey programs provided by major mutual fund families, such as Vanguard, Fidelity, or TIAA-CREF, the states determine their own timetable of declining stock allocation over time.

Chart 11.2 illustrates the declining stock allocation in five different aggressive age-based investment tracks as the plan beneficiary ages, approaches, and enters college. Despite all of these age-based investment tracks having the same aggressive risk label, there are some noticeable differences in their holdings at comparable points in time.

Chart 11.2

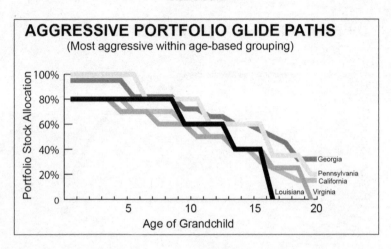

At the very beginning, when your grandchild has seventeen or eighteen years until college, the Pennsylvania plan has 100 percent of your assets invested in stocks, while the California plan only invests 80 percent. A larger discrepancy would occur on your grandchild's fifth birthday as California would reduce your equity exposure to 70 percent, while Pennsylvania would still be 100 percent invested in equities. The greatest difference would occur when your grandchild turned sixteen, at which point the Georgia plan would still have 50 percent of your assets committed to equities, while Louisiana would have none.

Of the states represented in the table, Georgia might be considered the most aggressive of the bunch, retaining a 32 percent equity position on your grandchild's nineteenth birthday and thereafter, while the other plans range between 0–20 percent at this point.

These differences aside, the most important investment decision by far that you'll make in establishing a 529 plan is whether you wish your grandchild's funds to be allocated in an aggressive, moderate, or conservative track. As will be further explained in our discussion about investment performance, over a ten to twenty year period, modest differences in stock allocations, like those noted above, have small impact on returns. However, the major allocation differences between an aggressive and a conservative portfolio have a much larger performance impact.

HOW STEEP IS THE GLIDE PATH?: While all age-based investment tracks are designed to become increasingly conservative over time by containing fewer and fewer stock holdings, the other element to consider is how smooth are the stocks-to-bonds reallocation transitions. Do the transitions resemble a smooth downward-sloping ramp or are they jolting, cliff-like changes? And why does that even matter?

An investment track that makes eight or nine modest readjustments over an eighteen-year period will have a fairly smooth glide path. The smoother your glide path, the less risk you have of stock-to-bond reallocations generating major value fluctuations.[4]

Let's look at a worst-case scenario. Suppose you have a grandson who was born March 1, 1993. Since you're committed to creating or continuing an educational legacy, you generously establish a 529 plan with $150,000 in your home state of Louisiana on his behalf. Ivy Leagues, here we come!

Now fast forward to March 2009. Your grandson just celebrated his sixteenth birthday and is beginning to think about college. But during the last eighteen months, the stock market has plummeted 54 percent from the heights it reached in October 2007. At that time, your grandson's 529 plan had reached $360,000 in value. During the last few years, Louisiana's growth track has had 40 percent of its funds invested in stock; so, your grandson's college funds have declined a significant 22 percent (40 percent allocation x the 54 percent decline) or a loss of $79,000.

But now that your grandson has turned sixteen, Louisiana will eliminate all stock in the portfolio in one fell swoop and switch to all bonds. Without any stock holdings in the 529 account, your

---

[4] Acheson, Leo; Holt, Jeff; Yang, Janet; *529 College-Savings Plan Landscape*, Chicago: Morningstar, May 26, 2016.

grandson has no way to earn back the $79,000 when the stock market recovers—which it did in dramatic fashion. The overnight allocation change would have made those losses permanent.

Admittedly, such an extreme example is unlikely. And as will be discussed below, over an extended time horizon, investment results tend to migrate toward long-term averages. However, the smoother the glide path, the less volatile or bumpy that ride will be along the way. Morningstar data indicates that allocation changes of no more than 10 percent are ideal for the smoothest possible 529 plan investment journey.[5]

INVESTMENT RETURNS

Should you just pick the 529 plan with the best investment return? No. The 529 plan investment decision with the most impact on your long-term future returns is the risk profile of your age-based portfolio (aggressive, moderate or conservative). In fact, spending countless hours analyzing different states' 529 plan investment returns with the goal of finding the best is probably a poor use of your time, particularly if you're investing over the long term.

Despite potentially large differences in year-to-year performance, over a long period (ten or more years), diversified portfolios with reasonably similar asset allocations will have very similar investment returns. This phenomenon is referred to as "mean reversion," or a return to the average.

In any given year, similarly diversified portfolios can have widely variable returns. For example, perhaps one portfolio contains more international stocks than others, or one contains more small capitalization stocks than others. As different investment categories go in and out of favor over the years, the portfolios will have significant differences in annual performance.

---

[5] Acheson, Leo; *College-Savings Plan Landscape*, Chicago: Morningstar, 2016.

However, over the long term, those cyclical differences even out, and the returns converge closer and closer the more time has passed.[6]

To illustrate this convergence of returns in the 529 plan environment, and as a caution against overanalyzing historical returns of different plans, the chart below shows the investment returns from four different aggressive growth age-based state plans at their earliest, or most stock-heavy, point in their glide paths. Specifically, the table is designed to show how much the various returns deviate from the average for different periods of time ending on December 31, 2017.

Chart 11.3

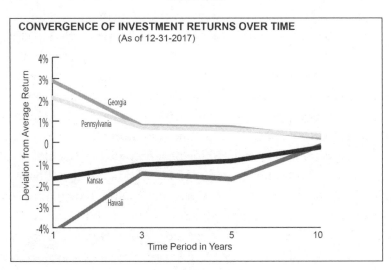

Looking back just one year, those four plans' performance ranged from a low of Hawaii's 16.4 percent to Georgia's high of 23.5 percent. That's a lot of variability for investment tracks all designed to accomplish the same thing. However, in looking back ten years, the average annual returns are tightly clustered around the average with very little variability. The lowest ten-year average annual return was Kansas's

---

[6] Mean Reversion theory was first discussed at length by Jeremy Siegel in his 1998 book, *Stocks for the Long Run*.

6.15 percent with the highest, 6.7 percent, belonging to Pennsylvania. The longer the time period, the closer the returns.

YOUR OWN TIME FACTOR: The last reason why an age-based portfolio may be the best for grandparents has to do with your own aging process. Let's take a hypothetical case in which the grandfather spent part of his career in the financial services industry and, now in retirement, investments are one of his hobbies. As such, he's opting to build his own 529 investment portfolio from a menu of available mutual funds. He's comfortable and confident in his ability to effectively manage his grandchildren's college funds. In fact, he and his wife just created a new 529 plan at the birth of their fourth grandchild.

So, what's the problem? Let's say our grandfather in this scenario is sixty-seven years old. If he insists on managing this most recent plan, he'll need to do so for another twenty-two years until the newborn grandchild receives their bachelor's degree. Should that grandchild pursue a law degree, our grandfather will be managing the fund for twenty-five years. That means he'll be responsible for the education fund's results until he is eighty-nine or ninety-three years old!

Obviously, he has no way of knowing whether he'll still have the inclination, the time or, frankly, the mental faculties to continue consistently performing so important a task so long into the future. With all due respect to Charlie Munger and Warren Buffet—who, as of this writing, are ninety-four and eighty-seven years old, respectively, and still effectively managing Berkshire Hathaway's $700 billion in assets—most of us lose a step or two at that age, whether we'd like to admit it or not. (Academic studies have found a decline in financial decision making capabilities and financial literacy as we age although, unsurprisingly, this decline has no effect on our belief that we can continue to manage our finances as well as ever.)[7]

---

[7] Bennett, David A.; Boyle, Patricia A.; Gamble, Keith Jacks; Yu, Lei; *How Does Aging Affect Financial Decision Making?"* Boston: Center for Retirement Research at Boston College, January, 2015.

A WORD ABOUT FEES

Fees matter! Over an extended investment horizon, such as the ten to twenty years during which your grandchildren's college funds will be growing, seemingly minor fee differences have a surprisingly large impact on the amount of money ultimately available for tuition. This is because their effect is magnified by long-term compounding. Fees' oversized impact upon long-term results is particularly true since investment performance itself, as previously noted, tends to converge toward strikingly similar returns over the long run. Luckily, fees are also one of the factors over which you have a measure of control based upon several choices you make about your 529 plan.

Fees in 529 college savings plans have two components: internal fund investment fees and state-level administrative fees. Internal investment fees are the costs embedded in the mutual funds or ETFs being used in your portfolio or investment track. You actually never "see" these fees since the mutual funds report performance net of these fees, or after the fees have been deducted from your returns. These fund-level fees include management, administration, and marketing costs incurred by the underlying mutual fund family—and they can vary significantly.

The second layer of 529 fees is what each state charges for the administration and management of their 529 savings plan programs. Again, these vary a great deal. Together, these two layers of fees create the portfolio's total expense ratio. To illustrate the wide variability in fees, according to Morningstar's 2016 Survey of 529 savings plans, fees ranged from the highest in Iowa's IAdvisor 529 Plan at 1.79 percent per year, all the way down to the Michigan Education Savings Program at only 0.17 percent per year. So, let's look at the two major factors, or decision points, influencing fees and their long-term impact on your grandchildren's college funds.

DIRECTLY SOLD VERSUS ADVISOR-SOLD 529 SAVINGS PLANS: Most states offer two avenues of access to their 529 plans. The first avenue is directly with the account owner. All dealings with the grand-parent or parent occur directly with the state. There are no middle-persons involved in assisting in this relationship. However, states also permit access via financial advisors. Plans sold through a third-party advisor entail higher administrative fees because the advisors need to be appropriately compensated for their work and expertise, which may involve plan selection, investment oversight, portfolio rebalancing, and funding strategies.

According to Morningstar, as of December 31, 2015, advisor-sold 529 plans had total annual fees ranging from Texas and Iowa's 1.79 percent down to Arkansas's 0.60 percent annual fee. (These states also offer the less expensive directly sold plans.) Most advisor-sold 529 plans fall in the 1.6–1.25 percent annual fee range. The fees for directly sold plans ranged from the District of Columbia's 1.2 percent annual fee, down to Michigan's 0.17 percent annual fee.

Those higher advisor-sold fees will undoubtedly provide a higher level of administrative service, but will they equate to better long-term investment performance? It's unlikely. As Morningstar states in its 2016 report, "Morningstar's research has demonstrated that more expensive investments are less likely to out-perform over the long-term."[8]

All that said, many financial advisors are able and willing to sell their clients directly sold 529 savings plans encompassing the lower fees, as opposed to advisor-sold plans. This is particularly true for financial advisors who are being compensated on a flat-fee basis rather than a commission basis.

Active investment management versus passive investment management: Active investment management involves investment managers selecting individual stocks or bonds. Based on their research, insight, expertise, timing, or temperament, they believe their buy-and-sell choices will outperform the overall financial markets.

[8] Acheson CFA, Leo; *College-Savings Plan Landscape*, Chicago: Morningstar, 2016.

Passive management, on the other hand, involves the creation of a composite portfolio or financial instrument to, as closely as possible, mirror the returns of a particular industry benchmark. For example, there are countless index funds and ETFs created to mirror the returns of the S&P 500 Index or the Dow Jones Industrial Average. Rather than trying to beat the market, they're simply trying to match it. Normally, the fees on passive management are considerably lower than fees for active investment management—usually in the 0.15–0.25 percent range.

Proponents of active investment management claim they can outperform the market, particularly in less efficient asset categories, such as emerging market stocks or small capitalization stocks. However, most studies indicate that only a very few active managers can indeed consistently outperform their respective benchmarks over an extended period of time.

S&P Dow Jones Indices conducted an in-depth analysis in mid-2017 to determine whether active investment managers across dozens of different asset classes, or investment styles and substyles, could outperform the respective benchmarks they were managing against. Essentially, for the ten- to fifteen-year time periods ending June 30, 2017, approximately 90 percent of active investment managers could NOT outperform their benchmarks.

The great irony of the report, from the standpoint of this 529 discussion, was the conclusion that the primary reason active managers could not outperform their benchmarks, or the criteria they were managing against, was because of their higher fees!

"IT'S ONLY ONE PERCENT—NO BIG DEAL!"

Can a fee that's merely 1.0 percent higher than necessary really make much of a difference? If the markets are going up, should you really worry over such a pittance? Well, over the long-haul, higher fees really take an oversized bite from your grandchild's savings plan.

Let's look at an example. Assume you established a 529 plan upon your grandchild's birth with $200,000, and the account consistently grew at a 7% annual rate prior to any fees being taken out. If annual fees were merely 0.25 percent per year, after eighteen years the account would have grown to $648,000. However, if the annual fees had increased to 1.0 percent, the 529 plan would have only grown to $570,900, and at 1.5 percent only appreciated to $524,300. That's $124,000 less available for college tuition than if the funds had been invested with the lower 0.25 percent fee.

A recent study conducted in early-2018 by C. Edward Chang, Ph.D., and Thomas M. Krueger, D.B.A., specifically examined the impact of fees on actual 529 plan performance.[9] Their in-depth analysis arrived at the same underlying conclusion: Even modest fees take a large bite out of long-term portfolio performance. At the end of their report, they concluded, "Whether one considers annual expenses or load charges, investors would be significantly better off to avoid paying such fees." Amen. Pay attention to fees.

KEY CHAPTER TAKEAWAYS

- Investing 529 plan assets isn't like investing for retirement

- Age-based portfolios provide a viable solution for most grandparents

- Check your plan's glide path

- Don't over-emphasize year-to-year performance differences between different state plans

- Over an extended time period fees have a major impact upon your results

[9] Chang, C. Edward, and Thomas M. Krueger. 2018. "529 Plan Investment Advice: Focusing on Equity Concentration and Fees." *Journal of Financial Planning* 31 (6): 34–43.

Chapter 12

Opening the Kindergarten Floodgates?

One of the most controversial and surprising components of the Tax Cut and Jobs Act of 2017 was a last-minute amendment buried deep within Section 1202 of the bill. Section 1202 contained a number of provisions meant to consolidate and simplify the numerous and confusing tax breaks for education savings. However, at the last minute, Texas Senator Ted Cruz inserted the "Student Opportunity Amendment," which contained a major change to 529 savings plans. Effective January 1, 2018, withdrawals of up to $10,000 per year could be used for kindergarten through twelfth grade private school tuition without penalty or taxation.

Prior to the bill's passage, such a 529 distribution would have resulted in a 10 percent penalty on gains and taxed at the account owner's marginal income tax rate. Unlike funds withdrawn for college, K-12 funds cannot be used for room and board, textbooks, computers, or other mandatory fees—only tuition qualifies.

However, the new tax law creates something of a financial paradox for grandparents with grandchildren enrolled in private school. Should you access 529 funds to offset K-12 tuition expenses? Is this a new and wonderful opportunity, or is it more akin to a Pandora's box better left undisturbed?

As of this writing, the vast majority of financial advisors urge caution because there are a great many unknowns, in addition to the amendment that adds more layers of complexity in planning for contributions, distributions, tax-related issues, and investment decisions. The following provides a summary of the four key considerations and possible courses of action.

SUFFICIENT FUNDS

The fundamental question for a grandparent considering use of their grandchild's 529 plan for K-12 tuition is whether there will be enough money for college. As previously discussed, college isn't cheap, and tuition rises every year. Depleting a 529 plan for grade school, middle school, or even high school, while leaving insufficient funds for college, is short-sighted at best. Certainly, from a career standpoint, it's college that makes the difference. I've never met a corporate recruiter who was more interested in a job applicant's grade school as opposed to the college from which they graduated. Ensure there are sufficient funds for college—that's the first priority.

LOST COMPOUNDING

A major drawback to K-12 distributions from your 529 plan is that in all likelihood, it will dilute the program's most appealing characteristic and the underlying incentive for its creation in the first place—long-term, tax-free compounding. As Chapter 11 illustrated, 10–20 years of tax-free compound growth enable the account to double or triple in value. The longer funds are left to appreciate, the larger the ultimate benefit to your grandchildren. Tapping those funds early for K-12 tuition, unless the account is immediately replenished, reduces that advantage.

Prematurely tapping 529 plans might reduce its long-term growth in a second, less obvious manner. If funds are needed near-term for K-12 tuition, most investment advisors would strongly recommend that some of the plan assets be conservatively allocated so that a prolonged market decline doesn't force you to liquidate holdings at the worst possible time, perhaps even at a loss. For grandparents utilizing an automatic age-based investment track, this would mean adjusting to a more conservative allocation, even if they're just entering grade school.

While a more conservative investment allocation will insulate your 529 account from any temporary market setbacks, history suggests that over the long term, its growth rate will lag behind a more moderate or aggressive investment mix. By withdrawing funds before your grandchild is of college age, you'll forgo compound growth on those monies. If funds are more conservatively invested, in all likelihood they'll be appreciating at a much lower rate, again diluting the tax-free growth benefit. That's a double whammy!

WILL STATES ACCEPT K-12?

All states must adhere to the underlying 529 tax regulations, whereby your funds can be withdrawn for educational expenses without any taxes due on the interest, dividends, or capital gains accruing in the account. Tax-free growth! However, thirty-five states and the District of Columbia provide college savers additional tax incentives (state-based deductions or credits) to make contributions to their 529 plans.[1] It's the future of those state-level tax incentives that are in question.

---

[1] Lieber, Ron, "Yes, You Really Can pay for Private School with 529 Plans Now," *The New York Times*, December 21, 2017, *www.nytimes.com*.

Will each individual state permit tax breaks for contributions that are shortly thereafter withdrawn for K-12 private school tuition as opposed to postsecondary education expenses?

Prior to taking action, contact your state's 529 plan administrator. A number of states will need to formally amend language in their 529-related statues as they specifically use the word "college" in defining qualified use of the funds. For example, Kentucky didn't approve the use of 529 funds for private K-12 tuition until July 14, 2018. Until those states make formal changes, a withdrawal from your 529 plan for K-12 purposes could trigger a clawback of the tax breaks you originally received when those funds were first deposited into the account.

As of mid-2018, ten states officially do not consider 529 distributions for K-12 purposes to be qualified educational expenses.[2]

SHORT-TERM REPLENISHMENT

One distribution-and-contribution strategy to both accommodate K-12 private school tuition withdrawals, while at the same time qualifying for state income tax contribution benefits, has been termed the "in-and-out" approach. Essentially, this procedure would call upon grandparents (or parents) to deposit an equal amount of money back into the 529 plan after K-12 distributions have been made. This approach would retain the total dollar amount of the account, thereby preserving its maximum tax-free compounding characteristics, while at the same time the contribution allows the 529 account owner to qualify for any available state income tax deduction or credit that is available for the contribution.

---

[2] Schoenberger, Chana, "How a Grandparent's '529' Account Affects Financial Aid," *The Wall Street Journal*, August 3, 2018, *www.wsj.com*.

As of this writing, several states have already put restrictions in place, and a number more are considering requirements that 529 contributions must be held in the account for at least 365 days to qualify for available state tax breaks. However, while these restrictions are designed to eliminate the most egregious exploitation of the new legislation (funding and then emptying an account over a few days), grandparents who already have a long-term 529 plan established and funded may still be able to take advantage of the short-term replenishment approach.

Wisconsin's revolving door restriction is a case in point. In order for a contribution to qualify for a state tax break, it cannot be withdrawn for 365 days. However, because Wisconsin uses first-in, first-out (FIFO) distribution tracking, a current withdrawal for K-12 purposes is considered coming out of your earliest contributions. As such, if you originally deposited sufficient funds to cover current K-12 withdrawals, you could literally withdraw K-12 funds and minutes later redeposit a like amount without running afoul of the state's revolving door restrictions.

There are a few things to keep in mind if you're contemplating a short-term replenishment strategy.

OVERSIZED ACCOUNT: If you funded your grandchild's 529 account at the maximum state dollar amount, or it has grown to exceed the state maximum, you'll no longer able to make contributions to the 529 plan unless its value falls below that maximum amount. In this case, your K-12 distributions will deplete the overall balance of the account. Work-arounds might include opening another 529 fund in another state and transferring a portion of the original fund into that new 529 plan.

THE SPIRIT OF THE LAW: Widespread exploitation of an unintended tax break in an already controversial 529 amendment may not be well received by state legislators strapped for budget dollars. In the aggregate, these potential state-level tax breaks for contributions that immediately leave the plan for K-12 tuition represent real money. For example, albeit a worst-case scenario, Indiana could lose $149 million in tax revenue[3] if parents or grandparents funnel the maximum allowable private K-12 school tuition payments through 529 plans. If legislators in cash-strapped states feel the system is being abused at their expense, these windows of opportunity will eventually be shut.

POSSIBLE COURSE OF ACTION

Prior to the passage of the Tax Cut and Jobs Act of 2017, the only tax-advantaged means of setting aside funds for K-12 expenses was in a Coverdell Education Savings Account. Parents or grandparents who may have Coverdell accounts for the benefit of children or grandchildren would be advised to consider converting them to a 529 savings plan. The new legislation has effectively made Coverdell accounts irrelevant. 529 plans cannot only be used for K-12 tuition, but the regulations governing them are less restrictive. Coverdell accounts only permit account owners to contribute a maximum of $2,000 per year per beneficiary. Additionally, households exceeding certain annual income levels are unable to contribute for that calendar year. Finally, Coverdell contributions must be made prior to the beneficiary (your grandchild) reaching the age of eighteen and used by the age of thirty. None of those restrictions apply to 529 plans.

As mentioned at the outset of this chapter, the new K-12 option with 529 savings plans add a layer of complexity to educational finance. And as will be discussed in Chapter 13, dealing with financial aid considerations, grandparents using 529 plans to help finance private high school tuition will materially reduce your grandchildren's chance to qualify for grants or scholarships. Grandparents and

---

[3] Malkus, Nat, "How the Republican Tax Plan Uses School Savings to Hurt States," *The New York Times*, December 19, 2017, *www.nytimes.com*.

parents should closely collaborate to create a long-term educational financial plan for the grandchildren to maximize funding and avoid unpleasant regulatory surprises. Whatever the approach taken, make sure there are ample funds for college prior to funding K-12. Higher education is the priority.

Key Chapter Takeaway

- Think carefully before depleting your grandchild's 529 savings plan for private grade school or high school tuition

Chapter 13

FINANCIAL AID AND 529 PLANS

In a typical year, federal, state, and local governments provide $109 billion in financial aid to students pursuing higher education. This figure encompasses student and parent loans, Pell Grants, along with government support. Additionally, government entities provide an estimated $16 billion in tax benefits in support of postsecondary education. And that doesn't even include an additional $46 billion that colleges and universities, particularly private schools, award in the form of grants and scholarships for students demonstrating either financial need or scholastic merit.[1] That's a lot of money.

Table 13.1 illustrates the percentage of first-year students at four-year educational institutions receiving grants or scholarships from either the federal government, state, or local government, or from the schools they're attending. (This excludes student loans.) Notable for this discussion is the high level of support from private, nonprofit universities: 82 percent of first-time students attending those institutions received grants or scholarships.

---

[1] Baum, Sandy, Jennifer Ma, Matea Pender, and Meredith Welch (2017), *Trends in Student Aid 2017*, New York: The College Board.

Table 13.1

Percentage of first-time undergraduate students awarded financial aid[2]
(Degree granting four-year schools)
For the 2014–2015 academic year

GRANT SOURCE	PUBLIC COLLEGES	PRIVATE NONPROFITS	PRIVATE FOR-PROFIT
Federal grants	37%	33%	72%
State/local grants	38%	26%	10%
School grants	47%	82%	31%

In the aggregate, this represents a tremendous pool of educational funds for which your grandchild or grandchildren might be eligible. But the 529 savings plan you establish on their behalf can have a sizeable impact on their qualifying for need-based financial support. Having a 529 plan will not automatically exclude your grandchild from receiving financial aid, but it requires coordinating your intended support with their parents and a bit of administrative maneuvering on your part as the account owner.

So, let's look at the financial aid landscape: what's at stake, how financial aid decisions are made, and how a grandparent's 529 plan can impact a grandchild's chances of aid from either the government or from the school they'll be attending.

WHAT'S AT STAKE FOR MY GRANDCHILD?

According to "The Condition of Education 2017" report, during the 2014–2015 academic year, federal grants averaged approximately $4,750 per first-year student recipient. State and local grants averaged

[2] McFarland, J., Hussar, B., de Brey, C., Snyder, T., Wang, X., Wilkinson-Flicker, S., Gebrekristos, S., Zhang, J., Rathbun, A., Barmer, A., Bullock Mann, F., and Hinz, S., Washington DC: *The Condition of Education 2017*, National Center for Education Statistics.

about $3,700. Both these amounts were consistent regardless of what type of four-year school the student attended. However, grants and scholarships from the schools themselves varied significantly based on the nature of the institution. Public four-year schools provided grant recipients an average of $5,700, while private nonprofit colleges' average grant was a bit under $18,000. The type of school in which your grandchild is enrolled or has been accepted heavily influences the level of funds that may be available. Typically, the higher the tuition, the higher the amount of potential school-based support.

PRIMER: HOW FINANCIAL AID IS DETERMINED

The Department of Education and educational institutions use a number of variables to determine how much, if any, financial aid your grandchild is eligible to receive. The key factor in their formulaic computations, and on which 529 plans have the most bearing, is the Expected Family Contribution (EFC). The EFC is an evaluation of your grandchild's (and immediate family's) financial status. Colleges and universities expect parents to contribute up to 47 percent of their net income toward the cost of college.[3]

Both the government and schools consider your grandchild's EFC, their year in school, the Cost of Attendance (COA), and number of siblings currently enrolled in postsecondary education to determine your grandchild's financial aid package. However, the government and most public schools use very different metrics and criteria to determine a student's EFC compared to private nonprofit colleges.

The Department of Education and virtually all public colleges use what's called the Federal Methodology. Financial data required for evaluation is acquired from the Free Application for Federal Student Aid (FAFSA) that the student and his or her parents complete. On the

---

[3] Onink, Troy, "2017 Guide to College Financial Aid, The FAFSA and SCC Profile", *The Little Black Book of Billionaire Secrets*, Forbes, January 8, 2017, *www.forbes.com.*

other hand, most private universities and a handful of public schools use the Institutional Methodology, which is based on data from the College Scholarship Service Financial Aid Profile (CSS Profile) that the student and their parents complete.

As you would imagine, the stronger a family's finances, in terms of both income and assets, the less need-based financial aid your grandchild is likely to receive, if any at all. While the FAFSA and the CSS Profile have notable differences in how 529 plan assets and distributions are reported and evaluated in making their eligibility calculations, the treatment of grandparent-owned 529 plans is particularly important.

FAFSA FORM: FEDERAL, STATE, AND PUBLIC COLLEGE AID

The FAFSA form is used by the Department of Education to assess eligibility for a range of government educational assistance programs—grants, work-study program, student loans—as well as by the vast majority of colleges and universities in the United States. Each year, the student must file a new FAFSA to assess their financial aid eligibility for the upcoming school year.

TREATMENT OF 529 ASSETS IN FAFSA CALCULATIONS: If your grandchild is considered a dependent of his or her parents, as reported on the parents' 1040 federal tax form, then they must include their parents' income and assets when filling out their FAFSA form (the same is true for the CSS Profile) until he or she does one of the following:[4]

- Turns twenty-four years of age

- Enrolls in a graduate program

---

[4] Federal Student Aid, An Office of the U.S. Department of Education, *www.fafsa. ed.gov*.

- Gets married

- Has a dependent child of their own

- Has been an active military service veteran

If your dependent grandchild or their parents are the owner of a 529 account, as opposed to the beneficiary, those assets are reported on the FAFSA. However, those assets are only weighted 5.6 percent in reducing eligible financial aid. So, for example, if your grandchild's parents had $150,000 in a 529 savings plan, your grandchild's eligible financial aid would be reduced by $8,400 ($150,000 x 5.6 percent).

If your grandchild is not considered a dependent of his or her parents and they are the 529 account owner, then those assets would reduce financial aid eligibility by 20 percent. However, if the 529 account owner is a grandparent, those assets are not included in the FAFSA calculations. Regardless of how large a grandparent's 529 account has grown, those funds are excluded from financial aid consideration. That's a real benefit! (But that changes dramatically once distributions are made.) Table 13.2 below summarizes the treatment of 529 assets based on FAFSA student aid calculations.

Table 13.2
FAFSA treatment of 529 assets

529 ACCOUNT OWNER	TREATED AS	AID ELI-GIBILITY REDUCTION
Dependent grandchild	Parental asset	5.6%
Parent of grandchild	Parental asset	5.6%
Nondependent grandchild	Grandchild asset	20.0%
Grandparent	**Grandparent asset**	**No eligibility reduction**

An interesting side note regarding FAFSA applications, albeit not typically the grandparents' concern, is that FAFSA-based financial aid does not include the parents' home, retirement plans, or insurance policies in their calculations. This seems counterintuitive, but the Department of Education does not want parents to cash in their retirement plans or sell their homes to enable their children to attend college. So, even if a family has an unusually lavish home, it does not automatically disqualify the children from FAFSA-related financial aid.

TREATMENT OF 529 DISTRIBUTIONS IN FAFSA CALCULATIONS: Here's where it gets a bit tricky for grandparents with 529 accounts, both in terms of how those distributions are weighted in your grandchild's FAFSA-related aid calculations and in terms of the timing of distributions.

While the funds and securities held inside a grandparent's 529 plan have no impact on FAFSA aid calculations, distributions weigh heavily against your grandchild's eligibility. A grandparent's 529 distribution in support of their grandchild is classified as student income in FAFSA computations, which reduces potential aid by 50 percent of the amount withdrawn less the grandchild's income exclusion.[5] Table 13.3 below illustrates FAFSA treatment of 529 disbursements based on the account's owner.

Table 13.3
FAFSA treatment of 529 distributions

529 ACCOUNT OWNER	TREATED AS	AID ELIGIBILITY REDUCTION
Dependent grandchild	Parental distribution	No Impact—0%
Parent of grandchild	Parental distribution	No Impact—0%

[5] The annual income exclusion is the level of student earnings exempt from financial aid consideration. Earnings beyond this annual exemption reduce student aid eligibility by 50 percent. The annual student earnings exemption was $6,570 in 2018.

529 ACCOUNT OWNER	TREATED AS	AID ELIGIBILITY REDUCTION
Nondependent grandchild	Grandchild distribution	No Impact—0%
Grandparent	**Grandchild income**	**50% aid reduction** (less income exclusion)

This isn't particularly straightforward, so let's walk through a hypothetical example. Years ago, a generous grandmother created a 529 savings plan for her young granddaughter. Now her granddaughter has been accepted to *the* Ohio State University. In an enthusiastic show of support, our grandmother intends to pay for all costs associated with her granddaughter's freshman year at school. Since her granddaughter currently lives in Michigan, she'll be paying the steeper out-of-state tuition. The COA at Ohio State for a nonresident to become a Buckeye is approximately $42,000. If our grandmother distributes that amount to Ohio State on her granddaughter's behalf, how will that impact her granddaughter's financial aid eligibility?

For illustrative purposes, we'll assume the granddaughter wasn't able to work during high school. The grandmother's $42,000 distribution is classified as student income for FAFSA aid purposes. So, the eligibility reduction is $42,000 less the student income exclusion of $6,570, which equals $35,430, which is then multiplied by 50 percent. The net result will be a reduction in the granddaughter's potential FAFSA-related financial aid by $17,715. That's significant!

However, the distribution's impact on aid eligibility is delayed for two years, which significantly lessens the potential adverse impact of grandparent 529 support. Prior to 2015, distributions from a 529 account were reported for the following year's financial aid consideration. For example, a withdrawal made in 2014 would have affected financial aid calculations for the 2015–2106 academic year.

In September 2015, President Obama signed an executive order to simplify the FAFSA process and expand access to federal grants and loans. A component of the executive order was that a family's or student's income reported on FAFSA would no longer be considered for the immediate following school year; instead, it would now be considered for financial aid two years down the road. So, for example, family and student income from 2018 would be used to determine financial aid for the 2020–2021 school year. Family and student income in 2019 would be used to determine financial aid in the 2021–2022 school year, and so forth.

This means that if a grandparent makes a 529 distribution for their grandchild, it will not impact financial aid considerations for two years. Reflecting back on our hypothetical grandmother assisting her granddaughter at Ohio State, the distribution in the granddaughter's freshman year will not impact financial aid until her junior year. Looking at it from a different perspective, if the grandmother waits until her granddaughter's junior year to provide financial assistance, her support will have no impact on financial aid computations at any time during her granddaughter's first four school years.

Additionally, due to the overlap between the calendar year and the academic year, grandparent 529 support can actually be made in the second half of the grandchild's sophomore year without incurring any impact upon financial aid calculations.

CSS PROFILE: PRIVATE COLLEGE GRANTS AND SCHOLARSHIPS

The CSS Profile is used predominately by private colleges and universities, in conjunction with the FAFSA, to gain a more complete picture of a family's financial capacity. (The Resource appendix in this book provides a link to a list of all schools that require the CSS Profile for financial aid.)

The CSS Profile accomplishes this in two ways. First, the form not only requests family income for the most recent calendar year just ended, like the FAFSA, but it also requires applicants to estimate their family income for the current year. This approach recognizes the fact that families with more complex assets and higher earnings can experience significant year-over-year fluctuations in their income.

But the biggest difference between the FAFSA and CSS Profile is that the latter requests information on a number of assets that FAFSA ignores. Most of those assets are added into the private school's financial aid computations. This includes equity in the family's home, nonretirement annuities, cash value of insurance policies, family businesses, and family farms, as well as trust accounts for the benefit of either the student of any of his or her siblings. The CSS Profile even requests balances on parent or student retirement plans, although retirement assets are typically not directly included in the calculations.

The CSS Profile also requests balances on any 529 savings plan, regardless of who owns the account, that names the prospective student as a beneficiary or which names any of the student's siblings as a beneficiary. However, while 529 plans owned by the parents or the student are part of the school's calculations, the funds held in a grandparent-owned 529 plan are not included. In this case, the treatment is similar to federal aid criteria.

Table 13.4 below summarizes the treatment of 529 assets and distributions in CSS Profile-based financial aid calculations. The largest FAFSA/CSS difference regarding 529 plans is the eligibility reduction for a dependent-student-owned plan. The CSS Profile financial aid reduction is equal to 25 percent of 529 assets versus the FAFSA's more lenient 5.6 percent reduction.

Table 13.4

CSS Profile treatment of 529 plans[6]

529 ACCOUNT OWNER	ASSET ELIGIBILITY REDUCTION	INCOME ELIGIBILITY REDUCTION
Parent of grandchild	5%	None—0%
Dependent grandchild	25%	None—0%
Independent grandchild	25%	None—0%
Grandparent	**None—0%**	**50%—less income exclusion**

GRANDPARENT SUGGESTIONS

If your grandchild will be applying for financial aid, there are several approaches you can take, or a combination of approaches, to minimize their potential eligibility reductions triggered by your 529 savings plan.

POSTPONE DISTRIBUTIONS: The most straightforward approach is to simply postpone your 529 financial distributions until your grandchild is at least halfway through their sophomore year in school. As mentioned above, due to the two-year lag between when 529 distributions are made and when they're factored into financial aid calculations, those distributions will have no impact on your grandchild's aid eligibility in their junior or senior year in school.

TRANSFER 529 OWNERSHIP: Consider transferring 529 account ownership to your grandchild's parents, depending on the account's tipping point. The tipping point is the point at which the financial aid eligibility reduction is less when parents own the account versus the grandparents. Essentially, you're trying to determine which of the two amounts below will be less:

[6] Onink, Troy, *"2017 Guide to College Financial Aid, The FAFSA and CSS Profile."*

- Parental 529 Plan:

    a) The estimated 529 account balance at the start of the year

    b) Multiplied by 5.6 percent

    c) Calculate this for four years, remembering to annually reduce the amount for each year's estimated distribution

- Grandparent 529 Plan:

    a) Determine the anticipated annual distribution for your grandchild

    b) Multiply that amount by 50 percent

    c) Multiply by two years, which takes into account the two-year lag

Generally, the larger the 529 account balance, the better it is to retain grandparent ownership. But let's take a look at two examples. (It's easier to determine the tipping point than it probably sounds.)

In scenario one, your 529 account balance is $150,000, and annual distributions will be $35,000.

- Grandparent owned: $35,000 x 2 years x 50% =$35,000 total financial aid eligibility reduction, or $17,500 each of the two years

- Parent owned: Year 1 $150,000 x 5.6% = $8,400
  Year 2 115,000 x 5.6% = 6,440
  Year 3 80,000 x 5.6% = 4,480
  Year 4 45,000 x 5.5% = 2,520
  total aid reduction $21,840

In scenario one, from a potential financial aid standpoint, the grandchild would be better off if account ownership was transferred to the parents. But let's look at another scenario in which the account has grown much larger.

In scenario two, your 529 account balance is $500,000, and annual distributions will be $35,000.

- Grandparent owned: $35,000 x 2 years x 50% = $35,000 total financial aid eligibility reduction, or $17,500 each of the two years

- Parent owned: Year 1 $500,000 x 5.6% = $28,000
  Year 2 465,000 x 5.6% = 26,040
  Year 3 430,000 x 5.6% = 24,080
  Year 4 395,000 x 5.6% = 22,120
  total aid reduction $100,240

In scenario two, from a potential financial aid standpoint, the grandchild would be better off if account ownership is retained by the grandparent.

There are a number of legitimate administrative reasons to transfer 529 account ownership to your grandchild's parents as distributions approach, but if financial aid is a major objective and it's a viable opportunity, it's worth crunching the numbers to determine your 529 plan's tipping point. In order to consider transferring 529 account ownership, make sure your plan is not based in a state that prohibits such transfers. As of mid-2018, the following states do NOT permit transfer of 529 account ownership: Arizona, Delaware, Louisiana, Massachusetts, Montana, New Hampshire, and Tennessee.

HYBRID PLAN: The third option is something of a hybrid solution. It would entail transferring a portion of your 529 plan, sufficient for one year's worth of anticipated distributions, into a 529 plan owned by your grandchild's parents. Since the funds only represent a portion of your total assets and they'll flow through the parent-owned 529 plan, the impact on your grandchild's financial aid eligibility will be modest.

Technically this would be considered a partial rollover and, as such, requires attention to strict administrative requirements to ensure the transfer isn't treated as a taxable event. Consider the following when making the partial rollover:

- Since you're only permitted one rollover to the same beneficiary every twelve months, it's important not to confuse the twelve-month window with calendar years. Suppose a grandparent did a partial rollover on October 15, 2020, and then another partial rollover on March 15, 2021. Although the two rollovers occurred in different calendar years, the two are only separated by five months. That error would make the earnings portion of the second rollover taxable.

- Rollovers must be completed within sixty days from the time the funds leave the grandparent-owned 529 plan. Miss the deadline and earnings are taxable. (This is why a direct transfer by the state administrator is preferable.)

- A few states have imposed requirements that funds be held in a 529 plan for at least 365 days to qualify for state income tax deductions. While this doesn't currently relate to rollovers, just to be on the conservative side, it would be prudent to plan ahead so funds can be transferred into the parent-owned account a year before they'll be subsequently withdrawn for school expenses.

As mentioned at the outset of this chapter, wisely accumulating a 529 plan for the benefit of your grandchild or grandchildren will not automatically exclude them from financial aid consideration, particularly at private colleges or universities. Incorporating the distribution and ownership strategies discussed above should enable them to maximize potential aid.

Key Chapter Takeaways

- Grandparent's 529 plan assets have no impact upon a grandchild's qualification for financial aid

- Distributions, however, will impact financial aid and must be made thoughtfully

Chapter 14

DISTRIBUTION AND
WITHDRAWAL STRATEGIES

The day has finally arrived! After years changing your grandchildren's diapers, babysitting, attending soccer games, school concerts, a few sleepless nights during their teenage years, and most importantly, wisely stewarding your 529 college savings plan (where did all those years go?), it's time to actually begin withdrawing funds in support of their higher education aspirations. Your grandchild has been accepted to their dream school. It's an exciting and energizing time for them. For grandparents who both encouraged higher education and established a 529 plan to help make it a reality, this should be a very gratifying and personally fulfilling period. Your foresight and generosity are going to make a significant impact upon your grandchild's life. But as to the actual withdrawal of 529 funds—where to begin?

There are a number of factors to consider to ensure the distribution of 529 assets is as advantageous as possible to maximize the funds' financial leverage and to make sure you don't inadvertently run afoul of regulations that could draw IRS penalties or hamper your grandchild's application for financial aid.

The following pages will address the importance of family collaboration; which higher education expenses are qualified for 529 distributions; the diverse range of approved educational institutions; the mechanics of making 529 withdrawals; and reporting and record-keeping recommendations.

Coordination

No grandparent is an island. Collaboration is the critical first step! Long before your grandchild's first tuition bill arrives, in fact even before your grandchild starts completing all those college applications and daunting essays, parents and grandparents should have a serious conversation about higher education finances. An initial discussion pertaining to the level of available funds and other potential sources of funding may have a major influence on which schools your grandchild chooses to apply to (private, public, in-state, out-of-state, four-year, two-year, etc.).

Conversely, you may wish to hand off this final stage of the college financing puzzle to your grandchild's parents. Whether you are motivated by declining health, are no longer interested in the responsibility, or you simply don't want to deal with the administrative details, account ownership of your 529 plan can be transferred from you to your grandchild's parents. In that case, you needn't be a participant in the financial strategizing process. However, if you choose to stay involved, there a few things to consider.

Coordinate tax incentives: In addition to 529 college savings plans, there are a number of other federal government tax incentives to help ease the family's financial burden. However, educational expenses paid for from a 529 plan are not eligible for these tax breaks because you're already receiving tax-free compound growth on 529 plan investments; further tax credits would be akin to double-dipping, or simply would be overly generous on the part of the U.S. tax code. The two federal tax breaks—American Opportunity Tax Credit and the Lifetime Learning Credit—are tax credits that directly reduce taxes as opposed to deductions that merely decrease taxable income. As such, it's worth a little planning to receive the credits and effectively reduce higher education cost. These were previously discussed in Chapter 8.

FINANCIAL AID CONSIDERATIONS: As was discussed in Chapter 13, college expenses paid from a grandparent's 529 savings plan weigh more heavily against your grandchild qualifying for financial aid than if those very same expenses were made by a parent's 529 savings plan. If your grandchild will be applying for a federally subsidized student loan via the Free Application for Federal Student Aid (FAFSA), it may be beneficial to postpone or limit your financial support during their first two years of college—assuming they have that flexibility.

WHICH 529 PLAN TO ACCESS: If your grandchild is in the enviable position of being the beneficiary of more than one 529 plan, perhaps separately created by both grandparents and parents, from which plan should distributions first be made? Or should they be accessed on a proportional basis? Considerations include the possibilities of financial aid, if either plan is approaching its respective state maximum contribution level, how each of the 529 plans are invested, and if there is a long-term educational legacy plan for either of the 529 plans.

HIGHER EDUCATION QUALIFYING EXPENSES

Qualifying expenses are defined as those costs that are required to attend any eligible postsecondary educational institution. Thankfully, that covers a lot of ground! So, let's look at what is and is not considered qualifying educational expenses for 529 savings plan distributions—including a unique opportunity related to housing costs.

QUALIFIED EXPENDITURES:

- Tuition and any mandatory enrollment fees. Tuition is self-explanatory, but mandatory fees might include student service fees.

- Books and supplies. Most schools determine an expected budget for books and supplies for a student based on their specific courses. It's recommended that your 529 expenditure for books not exceed the school's budget for this item.

- Computer and related equipment. As of 2015, thanks to the Protecting Americans from Tax Hikes Act (PATH), computers and computer-related technology are qualified higher education expenses for 529 distributions. Qualifying costs include the laptop itself, underlying software, and peripheral equipment, such as printers, internet services, and any specific programs related to classes.

- Food. If your grandchild purchases a meal plan whereby they'll be dining at school food service facilities, those expenses automatically qualify for 529 distributions. Food expenses also qualify if your grandchild will be purchasing their own food, but the qualified portion of those expenditures cannot exceed the comparable cost of a meal plan for the same period of time. So, if a student meal plan for the semester costs $3,500 at your grandchild's school, that's the most that can be offset with funds from your 529 plan.

- Rent. If your grandchild will be living in a student dormitory on campus or in off-campus apartments owned by the university, then their housing costs automatically qualify and are administratively straightforward. However, if your grandchild has other living arrangements, it will require a few added administrative steps to ensure all those costs are 529-applicable.

First off, for housing not owned or operated by the school, your grandchild must be enrolled in at least half the typical student course load to permit 529 qualification of rental expenses. Second, the rental amount can't be deemed excessive. Eligible educational institutions are required to calculate an official "cost of attendance" to provide guidance for federal financial aid purposes. As part of that calculation, schools estimate a reasonable expectation for room and board costs based on the surrounding community, the current time period, and for the student's general living arrangements. Qualified rent expenditures cannot exceed the amount determined appropriate by the college or educational institution.[1]

What about rent during vocational school or an online program? There is no specific IRS guidance on using 529 plan funds for rent if your grandchild is attending a vocational trade school or is enrolled in an online program. Some professionals believe that if a college offers online education and a room-and-board option for students who live on campus, then your grandchild should be able to apply the same criteria previously discussed for paying rent, utilities, and food from the 529 plan. However, this gray area becomes a bit murkier if the online school doesn't offer any housing. Check with your tax professional.

- Living at home. If your grandchild is living at home, his or her parents can charge their child rent, and said rent would be a 529-qualified expense. However, the rent becomes taxable income for your grandchild's parents.

Room and board expenditures during your grandchild's enrollment that exceed the school's own determination of what's appropriate are not qualified expenses. The excess

[1] If you're unable to locate this information on the school's website, contact their admissions or financial aid offices directly.

amount should be paid with non-529 plan funds or that excess amount could be subject to taxation on the portion of the money that are investment gains as well as a 10 percent penalty.

- Utilities. Utility fees, such as water, electricity, garbage, sewer, and gas bills, are all qualified educational expenses because they comprise a necessary part of housing. If your grandchild is living off campus, utility fees should be combined with rent expenses and then compared to the school's determination of total rent cost in their cost of attendance calculations.

- Mortgage payments. Faced with the prospect of paying four to six years of rent with nothing tangible to show for it when your grandchild graduates, some enterprising grandparents might consider purchasing a condominium or starter house for student housing during that period and later reselling it upon your grandchild's graduation. Under the right circumstances, those monthly mortgage payments would qualify for 529 plan payment. The key determinant from a regulatory standpoint is that your grandchild is actually incurring a rental cost; if so, those costs can be reimbursed from a 529 plan.

  If you or your grandchildren's parents were to buy a condominium and let your grandchild live in it for free while they were in school, he or she would not be incurring any rental costs. Thus, 529 plan funds couldn't be used as reimbursement for mortgage payments. However, if you or their parents purchased the condo and subsequently charged your grandchild rent, those rent payments would be qualified educational expenses—up to the school's cost of attendance determination. And you, as the owner, could take the rental income and use it to pay all or a portion of the monthly mortgage payments. In this manner, at the end of your grandchild's schooling, you have equity in the real estate.

This purchase-to-rent approach might also work if you helped your grandchild purchase the condo or starter house in their name, so long as they incurred a housing expense.

It should be noted that, in both this case and the living at home situation below, whichever family member is charging rent, which they use to pay the mortgage and housing costs, must report the rent as income on their tax return.

- Special needs. If your grandchild has special needs, a disability, or a learning impairment, any services or equipment they require for higher education attendance, such as a wheelchair or special transportation, would qualify. However, under these circumstances, it's wise to check with your tax professional. Special needs distributions from a traditional 529 savings plan, as opposed to a 529 ABLE plan (discussed in Chapter 15), could adversely impact any benefits your grandchild already receives from the government.

NON-QUALIFIED EXPENDITURES: The following expenses are not qualified expenditures and as such will trigger IRS penalties and taxation if paid for from a 529 savings plan:

- Transportation. Airfare, busses, trains, gas, and auto expenses do not qualify.

- Insurance. Medical, dental, or vision insurance premiums, as well as life insurance premiums, are not qualified expenses despite many colleges and universities offering their own insurance or group rates to students.

- Student debt payments. Student loans cannot be repaid with 529 savings plan funds. Common sense would suggest using as much of the 529 plan funds as possible so your grandchild incurs as little debt as possible.

- Electronics, smartphones, and electronic tablets. Any electronic devices for personal use will not qualify for 529 distributions.

- Various fees. Sports or health club activity fees, fraternity or sorority membership dues, or similar fees that may be charged to your grandchild, but are not required as a condition of enrollment, do not qualify.

- Standard of living choices. Other nonessential items include furnishings for dorm room or apartment, laundry services, or any other items that are more lifestyle choices than essentials.

- Computer software for games, sports, or hobbies are not qualified expenses unless their primary purpose is educational and directly tied to student course work.

WHICH SCHOOLS ARE QUALIFIED FOR 529 DISTRIBUTIONS?

The universe of approved educational institutions is exceedingly broad. These institutions fall into one of two groups: traditional and non-traditional. In all cases, the determining criteria for educational institution qualification is whether or not the institution is approved to participate in Title IV federal financial aid programs that are administered by the U.S. Department of Education. That criteria casts a wide net, everything from four-year private universities to online vocational training. The government's federal aid website, listed in the online resources section at the back of this book, allows you to quickly search to see if your grandchild's preferred education program is on the list.

In rare instances, schools may actually qualify under Title IV for inclusion in the federal financial aid program but have chosen not to do so. In these relatively infrequent occurrences, the schools will not appear in your online search on the government's FAFSA website. If your grandchild's potential education institution isn't on the listing, you can contact the school's admissions office directly to see if they've been approved to qualify for 529 savings plan distributions.

Traditional schools: Traditional schools qualifying for 529 plans include four-year degree universities, both public and private, community colleges offering two-year associate's degrees, and graduate school programs. Traditional schools are what normally come to mind when discussing higher education.

Nontraditional educational institutions: Qualifying nontraditional institutions reflect both the flexibility of the 529 program and the evolving landscape of educational opportunities.

- Vocational trade schools. Recognizing that a traditional four-year degree isn't the right pathway for all young adults, 529 plan distributions can be used for trade or vocational training schools. Approved vocational schools run the gamut from hair design to culinary training, fashion to film making, automotive repair to theological seminaries. Contrary to popular belief, many vocational trade schools are accompanied by a significant price tag. For example, annual tuition at the Academy of Interactive Entertainment in my home state of Washington is pegged at $18,300.

- International schools. Qualification of a great many international schools for 529 plans is usually a welcome surprise for parents and grandparents as students today seek broader educational experiences, whether that represents graduate studies abroad or simply in a single semester study abroad program. There are hundreds of eligible foreign colleges and universities listed on the U.S. Department of Education's federal aid listing. Approved schools include both the well known and prestigious, such as Oxford or Cambridge, as well as the relatively obscure, such as Jagiellonian University in Poland or the European University in St. Petersburg, Russia.

- Online programs. More and more traditional colleges are offering classes and degree programs entirely online. And while one can debate the pros and cons of little or no face-to-face interaction with professors or fellow students, online learning provides an efficient and viable alternative for students to learn from any physical location, at any time of day or night, at their own learning pace. Many traditional universities have made online learning a major emphasis, such as University of Florida or Arizona State University, while other institutions specialize in this approach, such as the University of Phoenix.

MECHANICS OF MAKING 529 WITHDRAWALS

Prior to requesting monies from your 529 plan administrator for the benefit of your grandchild, you'll need to find out when the money is due and decide to whom the checks will be payable.

WHEN QUALIFIED EDUCATION EXPENSES ARE DUE: The obvious first step is to find out when school payments are due and to plan accordingly. If this information isn't readily available on the admissions or financial aid section of the school's website, call either department to find out. Ideally, give yourself two to three weeks to account for the time it may take to liquidate a portion of your 529 plan assets. If you're not paying the school directly from your plan, allot sufficient time for a check to be mailed to you or your grandchild and for payment to be subsequently made to the school. It's awkward at best if you discover those tuition payments for which you've assumed responsibility are past due. Yes, you can always have 529 plan funds wired to your grandchild's school at the eleventh hour, but typically that involves additional fees, paperwork, and the hassle factor of coordinating both ends of the transaction at the very last minute.

TIMING: When requesting distributions from your 529 plan, it's important that the amount of your withdrawals match the amount of your grandchild's qualified expenses within that same calendar year. An annual mismatch between the amount of money leaving the plan and higher education expenses can raise a red flag with the Internal Revenue Service. The underlying intent of 529 plans is to provide tax-advantaged incentive to save for higher education, as opposed to providing a permanent tax-free investment product.

Consider a hypothetical 529 savings plan account owner who dutifully pays his grandchild's tuition during six years of undergraduate and graduate schooling from his personal checking account and then, after all that time has elapsed, cleverly reimburses himself from the 529 plan, benefitting from all those extra years of tax-free growth. That's not going to fly.

Ironically, despite the potential for abuse by aggressive 529 plan account owners, the IRS has not issued specific written guidelines on the annual matching of distributions and qualified higher education expenses. Nothing specifically addresses the issue in either Section 529 of the original tax law or in IRS Publication 970. Back in January 2008, the IRS announced that it was going to provide greater clarity to the annual matching or timing of 529 plan reimbursement payments, as well as allowing 529 payments made as late as March 31 to be applicable to expenses from the previous calendar year.[2] That IRS announcement clearly identified the potential loophole their omission had created. However, that specific guidance is, at the time of this writing, still forthcoming. It is widely recommended by financial advisors and tax professionals to annually match the distribution of 529 plan funds with your grandchild's education expenses.

WHERE TO SEND THE MONEY: You have four options regarding who will receive the distributed funds:

- You can request your 529 plan administrator pay the educational institution directly. Albeit simple and straightforward, this does require you—or someone—to follow up with the school to ensure payment has been received.

- The check or electronic transfer can be made out to the 529 plan beneficiary (your grandchild), who in turn would pay the education institution.

- The payment can be made to you, the account owner, and you in turn would pay the learning institution, and make reimbursements for qualified expenses made outside the purview of the school.

- The distribution can be made to a third party if they are responsible for making the subsequent payments on behalf of your grandchild.

Which approach is best? It's a matter of trade-offs. Obviously, you'll retain maximum control if all payments are sent directly to you. But is that wise? I strongly suggest that tuition, on-campus housing, and any other expenses invoiced by the school be paid directly to the learning institution by your 529 plan administrator. All other distributions should be sent to the beneficiary, your grandchild. Here is why.

---

[2] Hurley, Joseph, *The Best Way to Save for College: A Complete Guide to 529 Plans*, Savingforcollege.com Publications, 2015.

Making direct payments to the school is the most efficient option and eliminates the possibility of potential delays that arise when other parties—even you—are inserted into the middle of the payment process. In addition, if you, as the owner of the 529 plan, receive distributions as opposed to your grandchild, it can trigger unwelcome and unwarranted assessment notices from the IRS. When the state 529 plan administrator sends its annual distribution reporting to the IRS, it will indicate on the form that "the recipient is not the designated beneficiary." Because you were sent funds rather than your grandchild, it can generate IRS deficiency letters that authoritatively state that you owe a withdrawal penalty, tax on any gains that were embedded in those distributions, and interest, depending upon how long it's taken the IRS to send you the notice. Although those notices would be inaccurate, they require you to formally reply and provide all necessary receipts for your qualified expenses with your explanation. IRS errors certainly get resolved, but most would prefer to avoid the aggravation.

There is another ancillary benefit of making 529 distributions to your grandchild. If some of the 529 distributions are knowingly going to be used for nonqualified purposes, perhaps to buy a used car for your grandchild to use while in school, then it probably makes sense to have that distribution made to your grandchild. The IRS 10 percent penalty and income tax on the gains would be due from whomever received the distribution—in this case your grandchild—who should be in a much lower tax bracket than yourself. It's a good idea to make sure the parents are informed of the tax consequences of this plan because if your grandchild has significant unearned or passive income, it could trigger the kiddie tax, and he or she would wind up paying tax on the 529 distribution gains at surprisingly high rates.

Perhaps most importantly, however, is one of the underlying purposes of encouraging and supporting your grandchild's enrollment in higher education: helping them to mature as young adults and assume responsibility for their own affairs. Enabling them to budget, administer, and pay their own non-campus expenses can be another part of that process.

Once you've determined when to request funds and to whom payments will be made, it's time to request the distribution. Most state plans allow distribution requests to be made directly online, over the phone, by email, or by regular mail.

REPORTING

At the conclusion of each calendar year in which any distributions or transfers are made from your 529 plan, the state administrator or underlying financial institution is required to send a Form 1099-Q to the IRS. The 1099-Q form is similar to the W-2 form your employer uses to report your annual wages, or the 1099 form your investment manager files reporting your capital gains, dividends, or interest income for the year. Unlike the W-2 or 1099 forms, the 1099-Q recipient isn't required to report any of the information it contains on their 1040 federal income tax return.

The 1099-Q provides three key pieces of information. First, it reports the total amount of distributions or transfers that were made from the account during the previous calendar year, regardless of to whom the money was sent or in what manner it was sent. Tuition payments made electronically to the school or a small check snail mailed to your grandchild will be aggregated on the form.

Second, the 1099-Q reports what proportion of those distributions were the funds you actually contributed into the 529 plan, and third, what proportion of the distribution represents your earnings on the contributed dollars. So, for example, assume your 529 account balance at the time of distribution totaled $150,000 of which $90,000 was your contribution and $60,000 were earnings (60 percent contribution and 40 percent earnings). If you distributed $30,000, 60 percent, or $18,000, would be classified as contributed funds, and 40 percent, or $12,000, would be classified as earnings on the 1099-Q.

The administrative beauty of a 529 plan is that so long as your distributions do not exceed your grandchild's adjusted qualified higher education expenses, there are no reporting requirements for you, the account owner, or for the beneficiary, your grandchild. The earnings that are reported on the 1099-Q represents the tax-free compounded growth of the account. No taxes are due, and no additional reporting is required. You or your grandchild do not need to report your qualified educational expenses on any federal tax forms. (This is a refreshingly reasonable reduction in red tape on the part of the Internal Revenue Service, as even charitable contributions must be individually itemized on your federal tax returns.)

In addition to the IRS, the 1099-Q will be sent to either you, the account owner, technically referred to as the participant, or to your grandchild, the account beneficiary, depending on where distributions are directed. If the distribution is sent directly to the educational institution or to your grandchild, then it's your grandchild who will receive a copy the 1099-Q form. If instead, funds are distributed to you, the grandparent, then you will receive the 1099-Q.

Additionally, if you transfer some or all of the funds from one 529 plan into another, perhaps from one grandchild's account to another, you, the account owner, will receive a separate 1099-Q reporting on that rollover distribution.

Your 529 plan state administrator or the underlying financial institution is required to send the 1099-Q by January 31, so you or your grandchild should receive it in early-February. The Internal Revenue Service must receive their copy by March 31 if your plan administrator sends it to them electronically, or by February 28 if using a paper format.

RECORD KEEPING

While neither you or your grandchild are required to report annual qualified educational expenses, it is strongly recommended that one or both of you keep detailed records and receipts. This is particularly true for off-campus room and board, computer expenditures, or any expenses that aren't channeled through the school.

Each year, eligible schools are required to send both the student and the Internal Revenue Service a copy of Form 1098-T, which details all qualified educational expenses made during the previous year. This form is only sent to the student, so grandparents are relieved from yet another IRS-related missive. (Unless you're currently enrolled as a student yourself!) It is this 1098-T form from which the IRS originally determines the amount of your grandchild's qualified expenses for the year. It uses that figure to compare with any educational tax credits claimed by your grandchild or his or her parents.

Obviously, any expenses made outside of the school's purview will not appear on that report, and that, in turn, can create a mismatch between the amount of funds withdrawn from your 529 plan (reported to the IRS on 1099-Q). That mismatch may trigger IRS letters to you or your grandchild that there are taxes due on a portion of those seemingly excessive distributions. Maintaining detailed records and receipts will enable you to easily verify that all distributions made from your 529 plan were only used for qualified educational expenses and, as such, there are no taxes or penalties due on the earnings portion of those withdrawals. It is typically recommended that all records related to 529 plans be retained for seven years since you can be subject to the Internal Revenue Service's scrutiny for up to six years.

REFUNDS

Let's say your starry-eyed grandchild thinks it would be fun to take a challenging class or two well outside their field of study and naively enrolls in Quantum Mechanics or Kant's Philosophical Critique of Pure Reason. After several deer-in-the-headlight classes, they decide retreat is the best option—both to survive and maintain their grade point average—and they subsequently drop the class. If they don't sign up for another class, they will be issued a refund by the school for the class for which they paid but are no longer taking. If that class was paid for with 529 plan funds, at the end of the calendar year, you may have 529 plan distributions that exceed qualified expenses. That can generate additional taxes, penalties, and a few administrative headaches.

In the case of a school refund for a dropped class, or if unfortunate circumstances require your grandchild to withdraw from school altogether, returning the school-refunded amount to your 529 plan will eliminate any taxes or penalties. The IRS allows sixty days from the time the refund is issued to the time that amount must be recontributed to your 529 plan to avoid penalties.

NONQUALIFIED DISTRIBUTIONS (TAXES AND PENALTIES)

HOW MUCH IS TOO MUCH: To determine how much can be withdrawn from your 529 plan without incurring taxes or penalties, you need to calculate your adjusted qualified higher education expenses, or "AQHEE" as they're known in the 529 world.

Either you, your grandchild, or their parents should first combine all the qualified education-related expenditures your grandchild incurred during the calendar year (tuition, room and board, books, mandatory fees, etc.). From that dollar amount, subtract the following:

- Any tuition expenses that will be claimed by the grandchild or parent for a tax deduction. This harkens back to the government's distaste for double-dipping tax benefits.[3]

- Any expenses that will be used to claim either the Lifetime Learning Credit or the American Opportunity Tax Credit.[4]

---

[3] These deductions would normally be reported by the taxpayer claiming the deduction on Form 8917.

[4] These would be reported on Form 8863 by the taxpayer claiming the tax credit.

- Any costs for which your grandchild has been reimbursed by their employer's tax-free education assistance or if they have received veteran's assistance.

- Any tax-free scholarships, fellowships, or Pell Grants.

After deducting the above expenses, you're left with the adjusted qualified education expenses for the year. Your 529 plan distributions during the same year should not exceed this amount without you or your grandchild (whomever has the funds distributed to them) incurring income tax on the earnings portion of the excess withdrawals, as well as a potential 10 percent penalty on the earnings.

There are a few administrative-related errors that can also create a taxable situation on distributed earnings: not recontributing a school refund within the allotted sixty-day window after the refund was issued; changing the designated beneficiary on your 529 account to someone who isn't an official family member; and directing more than one 529 transfer or rollover within any twelve-month period if you haven't also changed the beneficiary.

A final trigger for taxable 529 distributions involves the termination of your plan because your grandchild has chosen not to continue their postsecondary education. If the remaining 529 funds are distributed back to you, the account owner, as opposed to your simply naming another grandchild or family member as a new beneficiary, income taxes as well as the 10 percent penalty will be due on the earnings portion of that final distribution.

AVOIDING THE 10 PERCENT PENALTY: Whereas the earnings portion of any 529 plan distribution in excess of adjusted qualified expenses will be taxed at the taxpayer's marginal income tax rate, (as opposed to the lower capital gains rate), not all such distributions are subject to the 10 percent penalty. Below are the exceptions that avoid the penalty:

- Qualified scholarships. Nonqualified 529 distributions can be made up to the amount of a scholarship without incurring the 10 percent penalty. As with all 529 matters, whomever receives the distribution should retain a copy of the scholarship receipt for their tax records.

- Long-term disability or terminal illness. If your grandchild should develop a long-term disability, or worse, a terminal illness, the 10 percent penalty is waived on excess earning distributions.

- Death. In the tragic event of your grandchild's passing and funds must be distributed from the 529 plan to their estate or to someone other than your grandchild, there is no 10 percent penalty.

- Education benefits excluded from income. If your grandchild is the recipient of veteran's assistance, financial support from an employer's tuition assistance program, or any education-related tax-free benefit, excess distributions equal to these benefits avoid the penalty.

- Attending a U.S. military academy. If your grandchild has been accepted to one of the five military academies (United States Military Academy, West Point; United States Naval Academy, Annapolis; United States Air Force Academy, Colorado Springs; United States Coast Guard Academy, New London; United States Merchant Marine Academy, Kings Point) where there is no charge for tuition or room and board, you can withdraw 529 funds equivalent to the cost of a comparable education without the 10 percent penalty.

Anyone old enough to be a grandparent has lived through the never-ending ebb and flow of U.S. tax policy. If you're just beginning the

529 savings plan journey, and your grandchild or grandchildren still have years and years before they'll be making decisions about their postsecondary education, you certainly understand that regulatory guidelines are not set in stone. As the days for distributions approach, check with your financial planning or tax professional to ensure you use the most advantageous distribution strategy in light of the rules and regulations in effect at that future point in time.

KEY CHAPTER TAKEAWAYS

- Grandparents must closely coordinate 529 distributions with grandchildren's parents

- To avoid penalties, match annual distributions with actual college costs

- Qualified room and board expenses could assist your grandchild buying a condominium or starter home

- Maintain detailed records of distributions and expenses

Chapter 15

"My Grandchild has a Disability!"

After the long-anticipated wait to become a grandparent, or perhaps just the anticipation for the latest addition to your growing brood of grandchildren, you receive an emotional phone call from your daughter or daughter-in-law. Your grandchild has been born with a severe disability.

Learning your grandchild has a disability, whether immediately identified at birth, a degenerative condition developing over time, or the result of a horrendous accident, invokes a number of emotions. Specialists in the field describe the normal grieving process grandparents experience upon discovering they have a special needs grandchild: shock, blame, sadness, coping, acceptance, and finally giving way to the actual joy of spending time with their grandchild.[1] But mostly, grandparents feel heartache for their grandchild and for the child's parents.

At that initial point in time, grandparents are needed more than ever by their children, the parents of the special needs child.

[1] "When You Have a Special Needs Grandchild," AARP, American Grandparents Association, *www.Grandparents.com*.

Grandparents can provide emotional support to the parents during an emotionally draining period. Grandparents can help relieve parents from their daily demanding duties. Grandparents can be an additional advocate for the grandchild since special needs children can't be their own advocates. But most importantly, grandparents can underscore that their special needs grandchild has been born into a family—and the family is in this together.

Beyond the all-important emotional support, grandparents may also want to provide financial assistance to their special needs grandchild for what will be an expensive road ahead. But that financial assistance must be undertaken smartly so as not to inadvertently disqualify their grandchild from government-provided programs. Herein lies the purpose of 529 ABLE savings plans.

BACKGROUND

On December 19, 2014, President Obama officially signed into law the Achieving a Better Life Experience Act, better known as the ABLE Act. Several weeks prior to his signature, Congress displayed a rare show of bipartisan unity by passing the long-awaited legislation 404–17. The ABLE Act amended Section 529 of the Internal Revenue Tax Code to enable disabled persons, or families with disabled family members, to set aside funds in a tax-free investment account (similar to a 529 college savings plan) that would not subsequently disqualify the disabled person from certain government assistance programs. Prior to passage of the ABLE Act, any of the estimated seven million persons living with disabilities in the United States who were receiving government assistance (Supplemental Security Income (SSI) or Supplemental Nutritional Assistance Program (SNAP)), risked losing those benefits if they attempted to set aside funds for their future needs.

Prior to 2015, once a disabled person's income exceeded $700 per month, or their total assets exceeded $2,000 in value, they faced serious risk of benefit disqualification. Assets included savings accounts, retirement funds, or essentially any items of significant value. In effect, this created a perverse incentive for persons with disabilities to permanently live below the poverty level. The only alternative for the family was to create a "special needs trust," which generally required a significant level of assets to justify the legal, taxes, investment management, and trust fees that accompanied such a trust.

As a result of the ABLE Act, eligible persons, or their families on behalf of the disabled person, can now establish a 529 ABLE savings account and benefit from tax-free compounded investment growth, while still qualifying for government programs. Since its original passage, there have been several legislative enhancements to the ABLE Act. Originally, disabled persons or their family members were required to establish 529 ABLE accounts in their home state. However, because many states were either slow to adopt 529 ABLE plans or never did, many disabled persons were excluded from the opportunity.[2] The 2015 Protecting Americans from Tax Hikes Act (PATH Act) eliminated the state residency requirement for 529 ABLE plans.

A few years later, the Tax Cuts and Jobs Act of 2017 opened the door for funds to be transferred from a traditional 529 college savings plan into a 529 ABLE account. This was an accommodation for when a disability developed after a 529 college plan was established. This latest enhancement may be the most beneficial in balancing the 529 ABLE plan's advantages against the Medicaid "clawback" feature.

Additionally, the maximum annual contribution for a special needs beneficiary couldn't exceed the annual gift tax exemption, currently $15,000. Now, if the disabled person is working, they can contribute additional funds above $15,000 from their earnings, up to the official U.S. poverty level of the previous year. For example, in 2018 the poverty level for a single person was $12,140. As such, the total potential contribution into a 529 ABLE plan in 2019 is $27,140.

Despite 529 ABLE plans originating from the same underlying section of tax code as 529 college savings plans and sharing numerous

---

[2] As of the beginning of 2018, only thirty states offered the 529 ABLE plans.

similarities, there are significant differences and several potential pit-falls grandparents need to avoid to maximize their 529 support of grandchildren with special needs.

529 ABLE PLANS—THE BASICS

The following describes the basic elements of a 529 ABLE plan.

TAX-FREE GROWTH: Like their 529 college saving plan cousin, 529 ABLE accounts allow after-tax funds (cash, not securities) to be contributed to a state-administered investment account. When funds are withdrawn to match qualified disability-related expenses, there are no taxes assessed on capital gains, dividends, or interest income accrued over the years.

WHO QUALIFIES AS DISABLED: In order to qualify as a beneficiary in a 529 ABLE account, an individual must be diagnosed with a disability prior to their twenty-sixth birthday, and the disability must be expected to last for at least twelve consecutive months. The individual must also be receiving benefits such as SSI. If both requirements are met, the individual automatically qualifies.

If your grandchild is not currently receiving government benefits but has been diagnosed prior to age twenty-six, they can still qualify to be an ABLE account beneficiary if they meet the Social Security definition of significant functional limitations and receive a letter of certification from a licensed physician.[3]

QUALIFIED DISABILITY EXPENSES: Qualified expenses include a wide variety of items specifically related to the needs of your disabled grandchild, and they are rightfully much broader than the

[3] "Able Accounts: 10 Things You Should Know," ABLE National Resource Center, *www.ablenrc.org*.

education-only-related expenses for traditional college savings plans. 529 ABLE expenses include:

- Education-related costs

- Job training or job support

- Health care

- Transportation

- Housing

- Assistive technology

- Personal support services

- Administrative and financial services

- Legal fees

- Funeral and burial expenses

Just like 529 college savings plans, distributions from your grand-child's 529 ABLE account for nonqualified expenses, even if inadvertent, incur the ire of the Internal Revenue Service.

The investment earnings portion of distributions used for nonqualified purposes are taxed at the beneficiary's marginal income tax rate in addition to the 10 percent withdrawal penalty.

MAXIMUM ANNUAL CONTRIBUTIONS: The maximum 529 ABLE contribution in any given year is equal to the annual gift tax exemption, which is currently $15,000. However, unlike traditional college savings plans, a special needs grandchild can only be the beneficiary on one 529 ABLE plan, while they can be named the beneficiary on numerous 529 college savings plans. While anyone can contribute funds into an ABLE account, those cumulative contributions cannot exceed the $15,000 figure in any given year. As noted earlier, the Tax

Cuts and Jobs Act of 2017 permits beneficiaries themselves to contribute additional funds, so long as they're working and not participating in their employer's retirement plan, up to the U.S. poverty level for the prior year.

This additional contribution feature has raised concerns with the disability support community. Their concern centers on the fact that 529 ABLE account owners are responsible for the administrative and record-keeping requirements to permit the additional contributions. And those administrative regulations are complex. Account owners are required to correctly track and report the different nature of their contributions. Mistakes could prove costly, potentially jeopardizing your grandchild's government assistance.[4]

In addition to potential government program disqualification, excess 529 ABLE contributions that are not corrected will generate a 6 percent excise tax on the overage, payable by the ABLE account owner. The excise tax can be avoided by an offsetting distribution made before the 529 ABLE account owner's personal income taxes are filed for the year in which the excess contribution was made. This can become a bit complex, as the correcting distribution must include any earnings the excess funds may have earned while in the account. Those earnings would be taxed as income but the 10 percent withdrawal penalty would not apply. Translation: Make every effort not to over contribute to a 529 ABLE account.

MAXIMUM ACCOUNT SIZE: Each of the thirty states currently offering 529 ABLE accounts has their own maximum allowable account size, just as they do for the traditional 529 college savings plans. The majority of states have established maximums at $300,000 or larger. Once an ABLE account reaches the state's specific maximum, no more contributions can be made to the account until distributions, or a decline in the value of the investments, brings the account level back

---

[4] Diament, Michelle, "Tax Law Brings ABLE Changes, Future Worries," Disability Scoop, January 9, 2018, *www.disabilityscoop.com*.

down below the maximum. However, this may not be the most relevant number regarding the size of a special needs grandchild's account.

If your special needs grandchild is eighteen or older, thereby qualifying for Supplemental Security Income (SSI), once their 529 ABLE account balance surpasses $100,000, those benefits stop. The first $100,000 in an ABLE account is exempt from the $2,000 individual resource limit that disqualifies persons from receiving SSI. Once the beneficiary's 529 ABLE account exceeds the $100,000 barrier, benefits are suspended until the account falls below that $100,000 threshold. (If your disabled grandchild has no other assets, the SSI disqualifying asset level would be $102,000.)

Other factors impacting qualification are distributions made for housing payments. These are classified as beneficiary income and may disqualify your grandchild from an income standpoint.

Although a large 529 ABLE account balance could suspend SSI payments, the account balance has no effect on your grandchild's ability to qualify for or receive medical assistance through Medicaid.[5]

CAVEATS: There are two restrictive characteristics with 529 ABLE plans that will influence how you might chose to utilize a 529 ABLE plan in support of your special needs grandchild:

- Contributions are irrevocable. All gifts or contributions made into a 529 ABLE plan are final. Unlike the traditional 529 college savings plan in which you can retrieve funds previously contributed, albeit accompanied by income taxes and a 10 percent penalty, that option is not available with the ABLE savings plan.

- State Medicaid clawback. In the event of the death of the 529 ABLE plan beneficiary, any funds remaining in the account must be used to repay the respective state for any Medicaid assistance the beneficiary received after the

---

[5] "Able Accounts: 10 Things You Should Know," ABLE National Resource Center.

account was established. In essence, the state becomes a legally binding creditor of the 529 ABLE account. If funds are still remaining after repaying the state, the remaining funds are distributed to the account's after-death designated beneficiary. When the final distribution is made to the successor beneficiary, they are required to pay income tax on the earnings portion of the funds, although the 10 percent penalty would be waived.[6]

SPECIAL NEEDS TRUSTS: Prior to the advent of 529 ABLE plans in 2014, grandparents wishing to help provide long-term financial assistance to a special needs grandchild without impacting that grandchild's federal benefit established a "special needs trust." Due to some of the more restrictive 529 ABLE governing provisions, these special needs trusts may still be a very viable option for grandparents with the means of creating a large safety net fund.

Special needs trusts established at banks or trust organizations often have a minimum account size of $500,000 or more, as well as significant fees for administration, legal and tax work, and the investment management. In a nutshell, a special needs trust will shield assets in the trust from SSI disqualification, and there are no maximum contribution caps or maximum account size limits. More importantly, a special needs trust created by the child's parents or grandparents is generally not subject to the state's Medicaid clawback process. And any funds remaining in the trust after the passing of the beneficiary can return to the establishing family members or other nondisabled successor beneficiaries specifically named.

Based on my personal observations over a decade of work within a commercial trust environment, special needs trusts are most commonly established in two specific situations. They are often established under the estate instructions of a deceased grandparent to

---

[6] Some states are prohibiting Medicaid clawbacks. On May 8, 2018, Maryland passed legislation prohibiting clawbacks from ABLE accounts.

ensure the long-term security of their grandchild. The other common event for creating the trust occurs on the heels of a major personal injury settlement, in which negligence by another party, be that an individual or corporation, has been the actual cause of the grandchild's disability.

Table 15.1 illustrates the basic comparable features between 529 ABLE plans and special needs trusts.

Table 15.1

Special needs trust vs. 529 ABLE accounts

ITEM	SPECIAL NEEDS TRUST	529 ABLE PLAN
Maximum annual contribution	No limit	$15,000 for nonworking beneficiary $27,140 for working beneficiary
SSI disqualification account level	No disqualification	$100,000
Tax on earnings	Sliding scale up to 37%	Tax free
Costs/fees	Legal, trustee, administration, and investment management	Minimal
Medicaid clawback provision	No	Yes
Maximum number of accounts	1	No limits
Administrative simplicity	No	Yes
Maximum account balance	No maximum limit	Varies by state ($300,000–$400,000)

USING BOTH 529 PLANS

The increased regulatory flexibility accorded 529 ABLE plans in the Tax Cuts and Jobs Act of 2017 provides a road map for one approach that would enable grandparents to provide their grandchild long-term financial assistance, benefit from tax-free compound growth, while at the same time insulating the bulk of those assets from the Medicaid clawback provision. That process would entail the following:

1. Create a traditional 529 college savings plan for the benefit of the grandchild.

2. At the same time, establish a 529 ABLE plan with your special needs grandchild named as beneficiary.

3. Each year, the maximum annual gift tax exemption, presently $15,000, can be transferred from the traditional plan into the ABLE plan without any tax consequences. Those transferred monies can then be used for the broader qualified expenses related to your grandchild's disability, while the traditional 529 funds can be used for their educational purposes.

Utilizing this dual 529 approach, a grandparent could maintain the ABLE account balance below the $100,000 SSI disqualification level, and the bulk of the assets contained in a traditional 529 plan could be reclaimed by grandparents in the event of an unexpected financial reversal.

A special needs child can be a daunting challenge for grandparents, but that grandchild can also be extremely fulfilling and rewarding. Providing some measure of long-term financial assistance is one of the many important potential roles a grandparent can play in the life of their special needs grandchild. The 529 ABLE plan can provide a framework to facilitate that support.

Key Chapter Takeaways

- Families can receive tax-free investment growth without being disqualified from federal disability-related subsidies

- State Medicaid clawback provisions and ABLE account limitations may make a special needs trust a better saving/investment vehicle

Chapter 16

PREPAID 529 TUITION PLANS

Prepaid 529 college plans are tax-free, state-administered programs guaranteed to lock in today's in-state tuition prices for future students. At the end of 2017, there were nationwide 1.1 million prepaid 529 accounts containing assets of $25 billion. Significant numbers although only one-tenth the level of total assets held in 529 savings plans.

Prepaid plans are intended to act as a hedge against tuition price increases that outpace a family's savings and investment returns. Like their 529 savings plans cousins, prepaid tuition plans are administered by individual states. As of mid-2018, there were eighteen state-sponsored prepaid tuition plans. However, only ten of those plans were still open to new enrollees. In addition to the ten state plans, there is an institutional plan overseen by a consortium of 300 private schools called the Private College 529 Plan.

Prepaid tuition programs are promoted as providing peace of mind. Once a family purchases future tuition units or credits, the state sponsor does the rest. The family can now rest assured that tuition is taken care of. The state offers a guarantee that a family's initial investment will be sufficient for college tuition when their child (or children) eventually matriculates. Families aren't burdened with investment decisions or forced to agonize over stock market returns. Once a child is enrolled in a prepaid tuition pan, the state does the rest.

This approach is particularly attractive during and immediately after steep economic declines. Not only do investments decline during recessions, but recession-induced revenue shortfalls often pressure legislators to reduce funding for state colleges and universities necessitating tuition increases, thereby squeezing families from two sides. Between 2001 and 2012, public four-year institutions reported that the percentage of total revenue generated from student tuition, as opposed to all other funding, increased from 40 percent to nearly 70 percent.[1] That jump was a result of reduced state funding and subsequent increased tuition.

However, like any service or product that assumes risk on your behalf, it comes with a price. In this case, it translates into administrative premiums above today's actual level of tuition. Most advisors believe 529 prepaid tuition plans provide the most hands-free approach but may not be the optimum way to save for college.

Let's examine how they work, their benefits, and their shortcomings.

Two Types of Prepaid Tuition Plans

There are two types of 529 prepaid college tuition plans:

Contracts: Under the contractual approach, parents or grandparents purchase a specific number of quarters, semesters, or years of college tuition. The price depends on the current age of the student and how the account owner intends to pay for the contract, either with a lump sum or in periodic installments. The younger the student, the lower the cost since the state has a longer time to invest your funds.

---

[1] Hemelt, Steven A., Marcotte, Dave E., *The Changing Landscape of Tuition and Enrollment in American Public Higher Education*, New York. The Russell Sage Foundation, Journal of the Social Sciences, Volume 2, Number 1, April 2016.

From a financial standpoint, tuition contracts are similar to a futures contract to purchase a commodity at some future point in time. You pay today's price for delivery at an agreed-upon point in the future. When it comes time for the student to attend college, the state administering the program typically makes direct transfers each quarter or semester to the school. Eight of the ten states still accepting new prepaid plan enrollees utilize the contract model.

Prepaid units: Prepaid tuition units are analogous to a hypothetical tuition index fund, the value of which increases at the same rate as tuition. In this case, parents or grandparents are able to purchase units that represent a fixed percentage of a year's worth of tuition. Typically, one unit equals 1 percent of a year's tuition. So, 100 units is equivalent to a full year. The price of your units will increase right along with the average in-state tuition composite your state uses.

Let's assume that our hypothetical grandparents living in Washington State purchase 100 units in the state's GET program on behalf of their newborn grandchild for a price of $10,000. Eighteen years later, when their grandchild is ready for college, a year's tuition has increased from $10,000 to $20,000. But because the tuition units they purchased are designed to mirror any increases in state tuition, our hypothetical grandparents can redeem their units for $20,000, which are then transferred directly to the educational institution.

Conceptually, both prepaid tuition contracts and prepaid tuition units provide innovative solutions for the ever-escalating cost of college. Unfortunately, a host of restrictions, limitations, and administrative challenges have made these programs far less user-friendly than originally anticipated.

PREPAID TUITION PLANS CURRENTLY OPEN TO NEW ENROLLEES

- Florida Prepaid
- Maryland Prepaid College Trust
- Massachusetts U.Plan
- Michigan Education Trust
- Mississippi Prepaid Affordable College Tuition Plan
- Nevada Prepaid Tuition Program
- Pennsylvania 529 Guaranteed Savings Plan
- Texas Guaranteed Tuition Plan (formerly Texas Tomorrow Fund)
- Virginia Prepaid529
- Washington Guaranteed Education Tuition (GET)
- Private College 529 Plan (formerly Independent 529 Plan)

GUIDELINES AND LIMITATIONS

RESIDENCY: Unlike most 529 savings plans, prepaid tuition plans require either the account owner or the student beneficiary to be a state resident. Massachusetts is the lone exception.[2] Nonresidents, however, are able to contribute to an existing prepaid tuition plan on behalf of the student beneficiary.

TUITION PRICE: Each state sets its own unique tuition price based on an enrollment-weighted average of in-state public college tuition rates.[3] Although most states have separate programs for their

---

[2] Flynn, Kathryn, "Prepaid College Savings Plans. Here's What You Need to Know," Savingforcollege.com, December 12, 2017, *www.savingforcollege.com*.

[3] "Section 529 Plans," FinAid, *www.finaid.org*.

community colleges and their four-year universities, a number of them do not. That can create some disparity in the return on your investment if you paid the state's weighted-average tuition and your grandchild decides to attend a less expensive two-year state school. As will be discussed further, that equates to paying a sizeable premium beyond what otherwise would have been required.

PORTABILITY: What if your grandchild's family moves out of state? If your grandchild attends college in the original state in which the pre-paid tuition plan is based, your grandchild can still use those units or contracted semesters. However, some states will now treat your grand-child as a nonresident student, and they'll require the student to make up the tuition difference between the resident rate, which was pre-viously purchased and locked in, and the higher priced nonresident tuition rate. That can be an unpleasant surprise. Fortunately, not all states offering prepaid plans take this punitive approach.

NON-STATE SCHOOLS: Another complication arises if your grand-child attends a private university or college in another state. Perhaps they're interested in a highly specialized field of study not offered in their home state, or they've been accepted to a private Ivy League university and relish the challenge and opportunity. In this case, the account owner, be it parents or grandparents, have three possible courses of action.

First, the account owner can change the account's beneficiary to one of the original student's siblings, assuming they have siblings. Second, prepaid tuition plans will pay the out-of-state or private school an amount equal to the state's weighted-average tuition for their state public colleges.[4] That amount cannot exceed the actual tu-ition amount in the out-of-state school.

The third option is the least advantageous. If for any reason you need to actually cancel the prepaid plan and withdraw your funds,

---

[4] "529 Prepaid Tuition Plans," Financial Industry Regulation Authority, *www.finra.org*.

most state programs will only refund your original investment or principle, possibly including a modest rate of interest. That forces grandparents or the account owners to walk away from what might have amounted to nearly twenty years of tax-free investment returns. That's a stiff penalty.

INVESTMENT MANAGEMENT: Prepaid plan account owners are not burdened in having to make any investment decisions. Similar to a retirement pension fund, it is the responsibility of state administrators to invest funds in such a way as to keep pace with tuition increases. Any unexpected shortfall must be made up by the state rather than the student's family.

CONTRIBUTION LIMITS: Since prepaid tuition plans are designed to support an undergraduate degree in a state public school, contribution limits are much lower than for 529 savings plans. While 529 savings plans have contribution limits in the $300–500,000 range, prepaid tuition plans are typically between $50–100,000. For example, Washington State's prepaid plan currently has a maximum number of unit purchases that equates to slightly above $60,000.

FINANCIAL AID: Prepaid plans are treated similarly to 529 savings plans, whereby student- or parent-owned accounts only reduce FAFSA-related financial aid eligibility by 5.6 percent of those funds. More importantly, a grandparent-owned 529 prepaid tuition plan for the benefit of their grandchild does not detract from aid eligibility until credits or units are actually redeemed for tuition.

TUITION ONLY: Prepaid plans cover only tuition and any mandatory school fees. They do not cover room and board, books, or requisite computer equipment. Families will need to utilize some other means of saving for these—potentially considerable—additional expenses. Some prepaid plans, such as Florida Prepaid, offer a separate prepaid program to lock in school-based dormitory costs. It should be noted that a family or grandparents can have both a 529 prepaid tuition plan in their home state as well as a 529 savings plan in a state of their choosing. The two college saving vehicles are not mutually exclusive.

TAX IMPLICATIONS: Any appreciation in the underlying value of your prepaid tuition contract or tuition units are free from capital gain taxes, just as with the 529 savings plan. Additionally, a number of states with state income taxes offer tax deductions for the purchase of prepaid tuition.

LIMITED ENROLLMENT PERIODS: Due to the contractual nature of most prepaid plans, there usually are limited windows for program enrollment each year. For example, Maryland's Prepaid College Trust allows enrollment between December 1 and mid-April each year. Enrollment on behalf of a newborn is allowed throughout the year.

PREMIUMS: In the past, prepaid tuition plans have been criticized[5] for having excessive fees and premiums, which has resulted in account owners paying far more than the actual price of "today's" tuition. While it's certainly reasonable for states to assess modest fees to offset administrative overhead, families seriously considering the prepaid tuition route should fully understand all potential costs to ensure no unpleasant surprises. Prepaid plan premiums take two forms: intended fees charged by the state administrators and unintended premiums that are determined by the school your grandchild ultimately attends.

- Intended premiums are fully disclosed fees intentionally added to the cost of your tuition contract. For example, when Maryland calculates the cost of their prepaid tuition contract, in addition to a host of assumptions, including

[5] Hurley, Joseph, McBride, Greg, "Does Your State's Prepaid Tuition Plan Make Sense," Savingforcollege.com, January 8, 2010, *www.savingforcollege.com*.

the age of the future student, the state adds 2.5 percent to the contract to offset operating expenses and another 2.5 percent to "support the actuarial soundness of the trust." That's an additional 5 percent for their plan. As of this writing, the purchase price of Washington State tuition units is 8 percent higher than their actual redeemable value. That represents a cushion for overhead and unexpected tuition increases. But unintended premiums are worse.

- Unintended premiums can be severe and are determined by the in-state school your grandchild chooses to attend. Remember, the contract price for future tuition is based on a weighted average of the state's public four-year schools. If the state has a wide range of tuition for its public colleges, you may get stung. Virginia is a good example. If you decide to purchase your newborn grandchild one year (two semesters) of future tuition, it will cost $17,650. That's going to look like a shrewd investment if your grandchild attends the College of William and Mary, which currently has tuition and fees totaling $22,044 per year. Pat yourself on the back.

  However, if your grandchild decides instead to attend James Madison University, whose annual tuition and fees total only $10,830, you've essentially paid a 63 percent premium for your grandchild's tuition. Not so good. At the time your grandchildren are in diapers, it's more than a little difficult to accurately predict where (or if) they'll go to college. In a state with large tuition differences between institutions, the possibility of dramatically overpaying adds a layer of uncertainty.

TROUBLE IN PARADISE

Despite the simplicity and hands-free nature of prepaid college tuition plans, they have a number of significant drawbacks. The most obvious is that only ten states currently offer plans that accept new enrollees, so you may not have the opportunity to consider their use. But the most concerning aspect involves the dependability of state guarantees.

The structural framework of 529 prepaid tuition plans makes them susceptible to the same problems that have haunted countless pension plans. Future outlays, for which the state is legally obligated, are based on economic and demographic assumptions made decades before the bills come due. And investments, also unpredictable, must be made in a way to meet those future obligations. The biggest wildcard in prepaid tuition calculations is the support level, or lack thereof, that state legislators provide to their in-state colleges and universities. If that funding precipitously declines, then tuition rises far more than forecast. As mentioned earlier, numerous states experienced this dynamic during and immediately after the 2008–2009 recession.

A number of states launched prepaid tuition programs with great fanfare only to find themselves in the uncomfortable position of being underfunded years later, unable to pay all those future tuition bills. Whereas states have responded to these shortfalls in a number of ways, including increased premiums and amended benefits, the most common solution has been to simply close programs to new enrollees, while still honoring previous commitments.

States that initiated prepaid tuition plans and subsequently closed them to new participants, are listed in order of closure:[6] Wyoming—1995, Wisconsin—2002, New Mexico—2002, Ohio—2003, Texas—2003 (since reopened), West Virginia—2003, Kentucky—2004, South Carolina—2006, Alabama—2008,

[6] Kantrowitz, Mark, "List of State Prepaid Tuition Plans," Cappex, June 28, 2017, www.cappex.com.

Tennessee—2010, Colorado—2013, and Illinois—2017. It reads like an obituary column.

Illinois is a regrettable case in point. In late 2017, the state suspended for the second time acceptance of new enrollees in College Illinois! 529 Prepaid Tuition Program because it lacked adequate funds to meet its future tuition obligations. The program currently has 38,000 participants. Between 2016 and 2017, the plan's unfunded liabilities increased by $56 million to $320 million and, as such, is anticipated to have only 74 percent of what would be required for future expenditures. This is somewhat puzzling in light of the significant increases in investment markets during this same time period.

While College Illinois! administrators work with state legislators to close the funding gap, from a strictly legal standpoint, the state is under no obligation to pay anything to fill the future tuition shortfall. That may not create a warm fuzzy feeling for enrollees living in a state with the lowest credit rating in the country—just one notch above junk bonds. As of this writing, the plan calls for honoring prepaid tuition commitments for those enrolling in college by 2022, but for younger participants, their families will receive a refund of their originally invested dollars plus any accrued interest.[7] However, based on the necessity to close the program, that amount will most likely be well short of in-state tuition.

The critical question for families residing in a state that offers a prepaid tuition plan is the nature of the state's guarantee. Only four of the currently open prepaid plans provide a guarantee backed by the full faith and taxing authority of the state: Florida, Massachusetts, Mississippi, and Washington.[8] Other states mandate a formal legislative process be undertaken to address any potential funding shortfall, but that only guarantees the process, not that the respective legislators

---

[7] Malagon, Elvia, "State Prepaid Tuition Program Comes to a Halt Again," *Chicago Tribune*, December 6, 2017, *www.chicagotribune.com*.

[8] "Prepaid Tuition Plans – Listed by State," Edvisors, 2017, *www.edvisors.com*.

will resolve the funding problem. For example, Texas shifted their guarantee responsibility onto the schools.

Most states' prepaid tuition plans are on sound financial footing. For example, Washington State's prepaid plan was 135 percent funded at the end of 2016.[9] The great irony was that the main selling point of prepaid tuition programs was to provide families with financial peace of mind. Yet the serial closing of prepaid tuition plans across the country may be doing the opposite, creating uncertainty for the families now dependent on them.

KEY CHAPTER TAKEAWAYS

- Prepaid plan limitations typically make 529 savings plans a superior option for grandparents

  - State residency limitations

  - Premiums and commissions

  - Underfunding and tepid state support

  - Much lower maximum contribution limits

---

[9] "Washington State Guaranteed Education Tuition Program," 2018, *www.get.wa.gov.*

Chapter 17

ALTERNATIVE FUNDING
VEHICLES FOR COLLEGE

There are a host of well-intentioned, government-sponsored savings and investment vehicles that are either specifically designed to support higher education or do so by virtue of their ancillary features. This chapter examines the four most common alternatives to 529 college savings plans and how they compare. We'll look at Uniform Gifts to Minors Act accounts, U.S. Savings Bonds, Coverdell Education Savings Accounts, and retirement plans.

UNIFORM GIFT TO MINORS ACT

It is a bit ironic that what used to be considered the go-to method for gifting educational funds to grandchildren a generation ago has become perhaps the least effective means of doing so today. The Uniform Gifts to Minors Act (UGMA) was established as a simple means of giving securities to children or grandchildren who hadn't yet attained the age of majority. Children who are minors cannot legally enter into contracts and, as such, cannot own stocks, bonds, mutual funds, or insurance policies on their own.

To create a UGMA account grandparents establish a custodial account at a securities firm or bank, typically appoint themselves as the trustee for the benefit of the grandchild, and then transfer cash or securities into the account. Those assets are fully owned by the grandchild but still controlled by the grandparent or trustee until the child reaches the age of majority, which ranges between 18–21 years of age depending upon the state. Once the grandchild reaches adult age, they legally have complete and total access to the funds.

However, for the express purpose of financing higher education, an UGMA account has a number of shortcomings, particularly in comparison to 529 savings plans:

TAXATION: A major drawback is that any interest, dividends, or capital gains in the UGMA account are subject to taxation. That can include the unpopular "kiddie tax," that, after passage of the 2017 Tax Cuts and Jobs Act, can quickly push your grandchild's income into the 37 percent tax bracket. Compared with tax-free income within a 529 savings plan, over an extended time period, this can be an extremely costly UGMA drawback.

IRREVOCABLE: The moment you give property to your grandchildren via the UGMA, the property is fully theirs. They own it outright. Unlike funds contributed to a 529 savings plan, you cannot legally retrieve those monies, even for life-threatening emergencies. As trustee of the account, you still control how those funds are invested, but it is considered a completed gift to your grandchild.

EFFECT OF EARLY DEATH: Even though your UGMA gift is considered final and complete, as referenced directly above, if you pass away prior to your grandchild's reaching the age of majority, those funds are added back into your estate for tax purposes. While they are still the property of your grandchild, your estate may get the privilege of paying tax on them.[1] On the other hand, as will be discussed in greater detail in Chapter 19, 529 savings plans are not considered part of your estate, even though those funds can still be retrieved by the grandparent.

UGMA FUNDS USAGE: Once your grandchild reaches adulthood, as early as eighteen years in twenty-nine states, they can legally do whatever they wish with the UGMA assets. Anything! Those funds can be used for higher education or to start a business, but those same funds, or a large chunk of them, could also be naively squandered. If your generous UGMA gift is made when your grandchildren are still in diapers, it's unlikely you'll correctly predict eighteen years down the road which grandchild will handle those funds responsibly and which one will not. This compares unfavorably to a 529 savings plan, where the grandparent account owner controls the account, even after the grandchild beneficiary reaches adulthood.

FINANCIAL AID: Funds gifted to your grandchild via the UGMA are considered your grandchild's assets for financial aid computations. As such, they will reduce your grandchild's financial aid eligibility by either 20 percent under FAFSA-based calculations or by 25 percent for CSS Profile-based calculations. If you transfer a significant amount to your grandchildren, your UGMA gift alone may disqualify them from financial aid consideration. However, if those same assets were held in your 529 savings plan for the benefit of your grandchild, they would have no impact on financial aid calculations.

CONVERTING UGMA TO 529: If you generously gave your grandchild or grandchildren funds under the UGMA with the intention that those monies would be used specifically for higher education,

---

[1] This would only have an impact on estates larger than the current $11.2 million exemption.

you're not stuck. The funds contained in the UGMA account can be liquidated and transferred to a new 529 account. Since those assets are still the legal property of your grandchild, the newly established college savings account will be an UGMA 529 account. Those funds can now grow tax free and avoid the kiddie tax.

However, the overarching UGMA guidelines would still apply. Once your grandchild reaches the age of majority, they have full access to the funds. And, similar to a traditional 529 plan, if they use those funds for nonqualified purposes, they'll face taxes and penalties on the earnings embedded in their withdrawals.

KIDDIE TAX: Prior to passage of the Tax Cuts and Jobs Act of 2017, the kiddie tax was relatively straightforward. Dependent children, potentially as old as twenty-four, were granted a modest level of allowable income for federal tax purposes. Once they exceeded that level, either as the result of wages or passive investment income, their tax rate was the same as the marginal tax rate for their parents.

However, under the new rules, dependent children are granted an income exemption ($2,100 in 2018) beyond which they must pay the trust and estate federal income tax rates. This revision may be even more onerous than in the past because trust tax brackets jump to the maximum rates much faster than tax brackets for individuals. For example, once your grandchild's taxable wages, short-term capital gains, ordinary dividends, and interest revenue surpass $12,500 for a year, ordinary income is taxed at the 37 percent level. By comparison, under the old kiddie tax guidelines, your grandchild's tax bracket wouldn't reach 37 percent until his or her parents had joint taxable income in excess of $600,000. That's a big difference.

A large UGMA balance that generates significant capital gains and income, even though earmarked for educational purposes, may have a large chunk carved out each year if the new kiddie tax is triggered.

U.S. SAVINGS BONDS

For generations, United States savings bonds have represented a no-risk, patriotic way to give money to grandchildren that would slowly grow over time. With denominations as small as $50, they were a convenient way for grandparents to give to grandchildren.

In 1988, as part of the Technical and Miscellaneous Revenue Act, the federal government deemed interest in Series EE bonds exempt from federal taxation upon redemption if the proceeds were used for qualified educational expenses. When the Series I savings bonds were introduced in 1998, indexed to inflation to protect bondholders from inflation, they too were made exempt from federal taxation if used for education.

Series I have become the most popular U.S. savings bonds as their interest is adjusted every six months in accordance to the Consumer Price Index for All Urban Consumers (CPI-U). In an earlier age, before the existence of 529 savings plans, before financial product innovation, before unusually low interest rates, and before tuition increases snowballed, U.S. savings bonds provided a viable complement to a college fund investment portfolio. But today, particularly for grandparents, restrictions and limitations make U.S. savings bonds a less-than-ideal investment vehicle for college savings.

GRANDPARENT RESTRICTIONS: The biggest downside is that the education tax exclusion for Series EE and Series I savings bonds is not available for grandparents! It only applies to educational expenses for yourself, your spouse, or your children. It would be available if your grandchild was also your financial dependent. However, if grandparents already happen to own a large portfolio of either of the two bond series, there is a legal work-around that enables grandparents to avoid tax on the accrued interest and reinvest those monies in what has historically provided superior investment returns, while ultimately using those funds for your grandchild's education.

The work-around entails establishing a 529 savings account in which you or your spouse is the beneficiary. Since a 529 savings plan is considered a qualified educational expense, Series EE and Series I savings bonds can be redeemed, with proceeds rolled over into your savings plan, without incurring any federal taxation. If your grandchild was the named beneficiary of the 529 plan, then taxes would be due upon cashing in the bonds. But since you or your spouse is named beneficiary, no taxes are due. After an appropriate amount of time passes, the account beneficiary can be changed to your grandchild.[2]

As with any rollover, the funds must be transferred from the U.S. savings bonds into the 529 plan within sixty days after the date of bond liquidation. Additionally, you'll need to complete IRS form 8815 to declare that you're rolling those funds into a 529 savings plan. Since you're taking advantage of a loophole in the tax regulations, while perfectly legal, make sure you check with your tax professional before implementing this approach.

EFFECT OF TUITION INCREASES: Even with the benefit of tax-free interest on savings bonds, your yield may not keep pace with college tuition. As of mid-2018, the yield on Series I savings bonds was 2.52 percent. And while interest rates are reset to keep pace with consumer inflation, the rate of tuition increases during the last few decades has exceeded the consumer price index. If tuition continues to increase as it has in the past, lower-yielding investments will fall further and further behind each year.

TAX EXEMPTION PHASEOUT: Since Congress intended these educational tax breaks to benefit middle-to-lower income families, the tax-free educational exemption on Series EE and Series I savings bonds is phased out when the bondholders' income exceeds a certain level. In 2017, once a couple's adjusted gross income surpassed $147,500, they

[2] Hurley, Joseph, *The Best Way to Save for College – A Complete Guide to 529 Plans*, Savingforcollege.com Publications, Pittsford, New York, 2015.

no longer qualified for the tax- free exemption. And once those modest returns are exposed to federal taxation, it's even less likely they'll keep pace with tuition.

This limitation can be particularly difficult for grandparents to correctly anticipate. The income restriction is based on the year in which the bonds are liquidated, not the year in which they are acquired. If grandparents are retired and derive most of their taxable income from investments, predicting their future income when their grandchildren are entering college is a difficult chore. Not qualifying for the exemption means paying income tax for all those years that you patiently held the bonds.

PURCHASE LIMITATIONS: Suppose you felt that Series I U.S. savings bonds were the best thing since sliced bread. You're planning to make a substantial investment in the bonds for your grandchild this year, confident that although the returns will ebb and flow with inflation, their education funds are inherently safe. Unfortunately, even if you wished to take that approach, you'd be stymied by the Treasury's limits on annual bond purchases. In 2012, the Treasury reestablished limits on the maximum amount of bonds an individual could purchase in any given calendar year. That limit is $10,000 per year, per bond series. Even if you and your spouse both made purchases for the ultimate benefit of your grandchild, the most you both could purchase together would amount to $20,000 per year in Series I bonds. That's a far cry from the maximum contribution limits for 529 savings plans that typically range between $350,000 and $500,000.

POST-1989 SAVINGS BONDS: The education federal tax exemption only applies to U.S. savings bonds issued after 1989. The ones that have been slowly accumulating interest for fifty years in the back of your safe deposit box won't qualify. You'll pay regular federal income tax on all that interest when they're eventually redeemed.

Qualified expenses: Educational expenses that qualify for tax-exempt savings bond interest is only allowed for tuition and any mandatory fees. Room and board, a computer, and any required books are not qualified expenses under this tax exemption.

The combination of limitations and restrictions outlined above make U.S. savings bonds a suboptimal way for grandparents to assist with their grandchildren's college finances.

COVERDELL EDUCATION SAVINGS ACCOUNTS

Born of the Taxpayer Relief Act of 1997 and named in honor of the late Senator Paul Coverdell, Coverdell Education Savings Accounts filled a useful niche in the pantheon of tax-advantaged educational saving options. Then, on Friday morning, December 22, 2017, Coverdell accounts officially became obsolete, or at least significantly less meaningful. That is the day President Trump signed the Tax Cuts and Jobs Act of 2017 into law. Among other things, that legislation expanded the definition of 529 saving plan's qualified educational expenses to include kindergarten through twelfth grade private school tuition, up to $10,000 per year.

Prior to that moment, Coverdell accounts were the only tax-advantaged savings vehicle that permitted K-12 expenditures. In reality, that was their only advantageous feature. Despite a host of restrictions and limitations, that one characteristic made Coverdell plans helpful for many families. Now that 529 plans qualify for K-12 private school tuition, it's difficult to rationalize continued use of Coverdell accounts, particularly when they can be rolled into 529 plans. The following table illustrates key Coverdell limitations in comparison to 529 plans.

Table 17.1
Coverdell and 529 comparison

FACTOR	COVERDELL ACCOUNTS	529 SAVING PLANS
Taxes	Tax-free investment growth	Tax-free investment growth
Qualified expenses	Postsecondary education and K-12 expenditures	Postsecondary education and K-12 expenditures to $10,000 per year
Maximum Contributions	$2,000 per year, per grandchild	Up to state account maximum, typically between $300–$500,000
Time limits	Must contribute by age 18 of grandchild and fully use funds by age 30 of grandchild	No limits. Most states permit 529 savings plans for perpetuity
Income limits	Annual ability to contribute phases out with income between $95,000– $110,000; or between $190,000– $220,000 for joint tax filers	No restrictions based on income of contributor

COVERDELL ROLLOVERS: If you currently don't have a Coverdell account for your grandchild, in light of the recent changes, most financial advisors would instead recommend use of a 529 savings plan. The 529 program is simply a better savings vehicle on so many levels. If on the other hand you already have a Coverdell account, seriously consider rolling those funds into a new or existing 529 plan for the reasons cited above.

WHEN A COVERDELL MAKES SENSE: That being said, there are a few situations in which it may be beneficial to retain funds within a Coverdell account. This is particularly true since you can have both a

529 plan and a Coverdell account for the benefit of a grandchild. If there's a high probability of your grandchild attending private school during their K-12 journey, their annual expenses will almost certainly exceed the $10,000 maximum distribution allowable from a 529 plan. In that case, having additional funds within a Coverdell account to augment the $10,000 annual 529 distribution would certainly make sense.

In addition, if you're bumping up against maximum account limitations in your 529 plan, a Coverdell account would enable you to contribute an additional $2,000 per year for the benefit of your grandchild.

RETIREMENT PLANS

What about using money from your retirement account to help grandchildren with college expenses? Although no data is available for grandparents, according to a survey published in 2017 by Sallie Mae and Ipsos Public Affairs, 5 percent of parents withdrew funds from their retirement plans to help pay for college, and 1 percent borrowed against their retirement plans to assist their children with tuition.[3]

The only case in which this approach should be considered is if you absolutely will not need those funds for your own use. Remember, your grandchild can always get a student loan as a last resort, but there isn't any such thing as retirement loan if you run short. However, if there are substantial funds in your retirement account, and again, you won't need those funds, then tapping them for your grandchild's education may be advantageous in some instances. Let's look briefly at the most common retirement accounts.

ROTH IRAs: Introduced by Senator William Roth of Delaware as part of the Taxpayer Relief Act of 1997, ROTH IRAs permit

---

[3] *2017 - How America Pays for College – Sallie Mae's 10th National Study of College Students and Parents,* Newark: Sallie Mae, Washington DC: Ipsos Public Affairs, 2017.

individuals to contribute up to $5,500 per year ($6,500 if over the age of 50) in after-tax dollars. The funds held in a ROTH IRA grow tax free, so when you ultimately withdraw funds, no federal tax is due. ROTH assets are ideal to assist with educational costs. Funds can be withdrawn, and by your paying the school directly, the funds are exempt from gift tax considerations.

While a ROTH IRA provides tax-free growth, like a 529 savings plan, because of the ROTH's limited maximum annual contributions, it would take quite a few years to accumulate significant funds. A final note: Your ROTH account must have been open for at least five years prior to withdrawal to avoid penalties.

TRADITIONAL IRAs: Traditional IRAs enable individuals to contribute pretax funds that then grow on a tax-deferred basis for as long as they're held in the IRA account. Upon withdrawal, those monies are fully taxed as ordinary income. Traditional IRAs often contain significant assets from either decades of savings or, more typically, corporate retirement funds rolled over into the IRA.

If nonretirement funds are available, it makes sense to first access those funds. Withdrawing traditional IRA funds will trigger federal income tax on the money removed from the account. If it's a sizable amount, it will likely push you into a higher tax bracket, which will increase your overall taxes and may severely limit many of your tax deductions and tax credits. Additionally, the longer those funds remain in the IRA, the longer they can grow tax-deferred.

A feature of traditional IRAs, albeit only applicable for those who were unusually young when they became grandparents, is that funds withdrawn prior to your reaching the mandatory age of 59 ½, but used for qualified tuition-related expenses, are not subject to the usual 10 percent early withdrawal penalty. (Income taxes will still be due.)

401(K), 403(B), AND 457 RETIREMENT PLANS: Conceptually, all these retirement plans are similar to traditional IRAs. Pretax wages are contributed into your 401(k), 403(b), or 457 retirement plan, hopefully generously matched by your employer. When funds are withdrawn, they are subject to federal income tax as if they were ordinary income. All considerations mentioned above in reference to traditional IRAs apply to these plans. They should only be viewed as a last resort tuition source.

If you're still working, these retirement plans will typically permit you to borrow from your retirement funds up to $50,000, or 50 percent of the balance, whichever amount is less. But does it make sense to do so for your grandchild's tuition? It depends. In borrowing from your retirement plan, you'll be required to pay a reasonable interest rate on the loan. You're technically repaying yourself, so the interest isn't lost. Whatever amount you borrow, those funds are no longer invested which, depending on your timing, could be a good thing or a bad thing. Most importantly, the loan must be repaid in five years, and if you are laid off or resign, the loan must be immediately repaid or it will be considered a withdrawal subject to federal income tax.

RETIREMENT PLAN CAVEATS: If you're considering the use of retirement assets for your grandchildren's higher education expenses, there are two factors to consider regardless of the retirement plan from which you're withdrawing funds:

- Financial aid. Distributions from a grandparent's retirement plan is classified as student income for both FAFSA-based and CSS Profile-based financial aid calculations. That will reduce financial aid eligibility in the following year by 50 percent of the amount spent on their behalf. While a grandparent's 529 distribution is also deemed as student income with the same 50 percent eligibility reduction, the 529 funds are given an additional year cushion before the financial aid reduction is applied. So long as funds remain in a grandparent's (or parent's) retirement plan, they are not counted in financial aid eligibility calculations.

- Investments. If you anticipate using the bulk of the funds held in your retirement account for your grandchildren's schooling, don't forget to adjust the asset allocation. Your time horizon for those funds most likely is measured in terms of decades. However, if your grandchild is approaching college age, those funds will be accessed in the near term. A long-term, stock-heavy investment allocation may not be appropriate if the funds are needed in the next twelve to eighteen months. A steep correction in the securities markets might force you to liquidate securities that have materially declined. Since those funds no longer have an extended time period to bounce back, you could significantly reduce the support you'd hoped to provide your grandchild or grandchildren.

While there are numerous tax-advantaged saving and investment vehicles that provide benefits towards building your grandchildren's educational fund, none have the scope of benefits, flexibility, and growth potential of 529 college savings plans. As the name of this book implies, I strongly recommend channeling your educational generosity through 529 plans.

KEY CHAPTER TAKEAWAYS

- Other saving and investment vehicles provide lass flexibility than 529 plans

    - Uniform Gift to Minor Accounts (taxable and irrevocable)

    - U.S. Savings Bonds (only available for parents with low annual maximums)

    - Coverdell savings accounts (low annual maximums)

    - Retirement plans (taxation and financial aid impact)

Chapter 18

SELECTING YOUR GRANDHILD'S 529 PLAN

Choosing the best state in which to establish your grandchildren's 529 plan requires a bit of research, as opposed to simply selecting your home state's plan. That's not to say your home state's plan couldn't wind up being your best choice. Optimum selection requires prioritizing plan features with your personal circumstances and then surveying the 529 marketplace in light of those priorities. The surveying aspect has been made much easier thanks to a number of website-based 529 search-and-comparison tools. Two of the best include *www.savingforcollege.com* and the College Savings Plan Network site, *www.collegesavings.org*. Both include comparison tools that enable grandparents (or anyone) to compare features among all state 529 college savings plans. But first, you'll need to determine which characteristics are most important for you.

PRIORITIZE ACCOUNT FEATURES

If you're establishing an account for a grandchild, your funding strategy will determine which features are most important. Remember, the objective is to maximize available funds for your grandchild's education. If there are funds left over after a grandchild finishes their postsecondary education, that's a good problem. Excess funds can be transferred to another family member's 529 plan, or funds can be distributed back to you, the account owner.

Below are four 529 funding strategies and the resulting prioritization of features for plan selection.

1. Maximum contribution: You plan to contribute the state's maximum contribution amount right from the start. The key considerations in order of importance will be:

    *   Maximum contribution amount. State maximums range from $235,000 to $520,000. If you're financially able to take this approach, the higher amount will provide the greatest education flexibility for your grandchild.

    *   Low fees. As noted earlier, the longer your 529 plan has to grow, the bigger the impact from seemingly minor fee reductions. Prioritize state plans with the lowest possible fees.

    *   Transferability of account ownership. Can you transfer account ownership? Make sure account ownership can be transferred prior to the death of the account owner. There are a number of reasons you may wish to pass the oversight baton as your grandchild approaches college age.

    *   Glide path. What's the age-based glide path of the state's investment portfolios?

    *   Residency requirement. Are you or your grandchild required to be residents of the state in which the 529 plan is based? People move.

- State income tax deduction/credit. If your own state passes the above screening and it has a state income tax deduction or credit available for your contributions, that's icing on the cake. Remember, in the big picture, tax deductions are very minor considerations compared to low fees and investment returns over an extended time period.

2. One-time lump-sum amount: You plan to fund your 529 plan with a one-time lump-sum amount, but it will be less than $250,000. After eliminating maximum contribution limits as a consideration, because you won't initially be bumping up against those restrictions, the prioritization of features mirror those above:

   - Low fees

   - Transferability of account ownership

   - The age-based glide path

   - Residency requirement

   - State income tax deduction/credits

3. Stacked contributions: You plan to fund your grandchild's 529 plan with stacked or super funding contributions that aggregate five years of the annual amount exempt from gift taxes. In 2018, that equates to $75,000 for an individual or $150,000 for a couple. You plan to do the very same thing again in six years:

   - Low fees

   - The age-based glide path

   - Maximum contribution amount. If the market enjoys consistent appreciation after your initial $150,000 contribution, five years later when you plan to repeat

the process, you may be limited by the account maximum if you picked a state with one of the lower
maximum account contribution levels.

- State income tax deduction/credit. Since you'll be
contributing funds over an extended time period,
give greater consideration to those home state income
tax deductions, if available. This shouldn't overweight
the above issues, but it's a possible benefit to consider.

- Residency requirement

- Transferability of account ownership

4. Periodic contributions: You'll be making unpredictable periodic contributions to your grandchild's 529
plan that in total will be far less than any of the state's
maximums:

- State tax deduction/credit. With moderate contributions spread out over individual years, state income
tax deductions or credits take on oversized importance, perhaps more than making up for slightly
higher fees.

- Residency requirement. If you're seeking state tax
deductions, you'll need to open the account in your
home state.

- The age-based glide path

- Low fees

- Transferability of account ownership

REVIEW THE PLAN'S DISCLOSURE DOCUMENT

Once you select the state 529 plan that meets your prioritized criteria, take the time to read the plan's disclosure statement. Granted,

this is not scintillating stuff, with much of it legal boilerplate, but it's worth double-checking the most crucial elements in your selection criteria. While you can always transfer or roll over the account into another state's plan, the intent is that this is the start of a long-term relationship.

Opening the 529 Account

Once you've selected the state that offers the 529 savings plan that best meets your priorities, the next step is to open your account. Beyond contact information, social security numbers, and the like, you'll need to decide on three factors at the outset:

Select your 529 account beneficiary (student): This will probably be your grandchild unless you're creating a surplus account for the eventual benefit of great-grandchildren. In that case, your beneficiary would be a family member serving as a placeholder until the birth of the next generation. Beneficiaries can be easily changed to other family members.

Select an investment option: As discussed in Chapter 11, if the account is for a specific grandchild, seriously consider an age-based portfolio that becomes less volatile or more conservative as your grandchild approaches college age. Most states offer three age-based risk profile portfolios from which to choose: conservative, moderate, or aggressive.

If the plan or plans are intended for even longer term—for educational support beyond your grandchildren—consider a static portfolio with a growth orientation. A static portfolio maintains the same asset allocation or risk profile regardless of the age of the future beneficiaries.

Select a successor owner for your 529 account: This often isn't immediately required to open the 529 savings plan, but it's strongly recommended. A well-chosen successor, be that a responsible family member or professional fiduciary, can ensure the continuation of your educational legacy plans. Since the successor can be easily changed should conditions warrant a replacement, it makes sense to initially identify your ultimate replacement.

If you should pass away without a named successor, the 529 funds may pass through your estate to the executor and then to your estate beneficiaries per the terms of your will. If you pass away without a will, the 529 funds will be distributed to spouse and family members in accordance with state law. Both of those outcomes may have absolutely no similarity with the educational plans you have in mind for your grandchildren. Identify a successor when you first open the account.

Funding the Account

Most states are extremely flexible in how they'll accept contributions to your 529 savings plan—just so long as it's cash. Securities or other assets cannot be transferred to your account without first being liquidated. Once you've done that, you can transfer those monies in numerous ways:

- Electronic bank transfer directly from your bank or investment account, either as a one-time event or automatic scheduled transfers

- Mail a check payable to your state's 529 savings program

- Wire funds from a bank or investment account (this typically incurs fees at both ends)

- Contributions from an Education Savings Account (ESA), such as a Coverdell savings account, without incurring any income tax ramifications on gains

- Liquidate Series EE or Series I U.S. Savings Bonds without income tax ramifications on gains or accrued interest

- Roll over funds from another state's 529 savings plan

- If you're still working, many of the larger plans can establish direct payroll deductions.

- Contributions can be made from a Uniform Gifts to Minors Account (UGMA), although the restrictions and characteristics accompany those funds.

Congratulations! You've successfully opened a 529 savings account for your grandchild. But what if a year or two after carefully and thoughtfully selecting a state plan, you realize you've made a mistake. Perhaps administration service is intolerable or investment performance proves mundane and lackluster. What then? No need to worry. You're not trapped in an unsatisfactory plan. If you can't resolve frustrations with your current 529 savings plan, you can transfer those funds to a different state's plan.

So relax. You've taken the first step in creating a family educational legacy. Now you can concentrate on the really important task: nurturing and encouraging those grandchildren.

Table 18.1
529 College Savings Plan Websites

STATE	WEBSITE
Alabama	www.collegecounts529.com
Alaska	www.uacollegesavings.com/public/ua529
Arizona	www.fidelity.com/529-plans/arizona
Arkansas	www.arkansas529.org
California	www.scholarshare529.com
Colorado	www.collegeinvest.org/529-savings-plans/direct-portfolio/

STATE	WEBSITE
Connecticut	www.aboutchet.com/
Delaware	www.fidelity.com/529-plans/delaware
Florida	www.myfloridaprepaid.com
Georgia	www.path2college529.com
Hawaii	www.hi529.com
Idaho	www.idsaves.org
Illinois	www.brightstartsavings.com
Indiana	www.collegechoicedirect.com
Iowa	www.collegesavingsiowa.com
Kansas	www.learningquest.com
Kentucky	www.kysaves.com
Louisiana	www.startsaving.la.gov
Maine	www.nextgenforme.com
Maryland	www.maryland529.com
Massachusetts	www.mefa.org/products/u-fund-college-investing-plan
Michigan	www.misaves.com
Minnesota	www.mnsaves.org
Mississippi	www.treasurerlynnfitch.ms.gov/ms529/Pages/default.aspx
Missouri	www.missourimost.org
Montana	www.achievemontana.com
Nebraska	www.nest529direct.com
Nevada	www.nevadatreasurer.gov/CollegeSavings/CSP_Home
New Hampshire	www.nh.gov/treasury/college-savings/unique.htm
New Jersey	www.njbest529.com
New Mexico	www.theeducationplan.com
New York	www.nysaves.org
North Carolina	www.cfnc.org
North Dakota	www.collegesave4u.com
Ohio	www.collegeadvantage.com

STATE	WEBSITE
Oklahoma	www.ok4saving.org
Oregon	www.oregoncollegesavings.com
Pennsylvania	www.pa529.com
Rhode Island	www.collegeboundsaver.com
South Carolina	https://futurescholar.com
South Dakota	www.collegeaccess529.com
Tennessee	www.tnstars.com
Texas	www.texascollegesavings.com
Utah	https://my529.org/
Vermont	www.vheip.org
Virginia	www.virginia529.com
Washington	www.dreamahead.wa.gov
West Virginia	www.smart529.com
Wisconsin	www.edvest.com
District of Columbia	www.dccollegesavings.com

Key Chapter Takeaways

- Your 529 funding strategy will determine which features to prioritize in plan selection

- Use online comparison tools to evaluate different state plan features

Chapter 19

529 ESTATE PLANNING ISSUES

The primary role of your 529 college savings plan is to assist your grandchildren, or anyone of your choosing, with the costs of their postsecondary education. That should be the overwhelming priority in considering whether to establish a 529 account. However, due to combination of unique features and regulatory flexibility, 529 plans can be an effective tool to minimize the tax impact in the disposition of your estate.

UNIQUE FEATURES

Perhaps the most unique feature of 529 college savings plans is the regulatory treatment of contributions, and any subsequent earnings on those contributions, as completed gifts. This is the case despite the fact that grandparents, or any account owner, still controls those funds, directs how they're invested, and can even retrieve them, albeit with tax and penalty, should the need arise.[1] As a result, any funds contributed to a 529 plan are legally removed from your estate.

---

[1] Technically 529 contributions are considered a "completed gift of a present interest," as opposed to a "contingent gift of a future interest."

In virtually all other areas of tax or estate law, if an individual making a gift or contribution retains control, or has any means of reclaiming those assets however tenuous, those assets are included back into the individual's estate when they pass. Some provisions even add assets back into a taxable estate if the transfer was made within two years before the date of death.

Another favorable 529 savings plan characteristic is the ability to "super fund," or accelerate five years of gift tax exclusion contributions into a single year. With the current annual gift exclusion level at $15,000 per spouse, per recipient, this 529 accelerating feature enables an individual to give up to $75,000 per year to as many persons as they desire, or a couple can give up to $150,000 per year to as many persons as they desire, via 529 plans without those dollars counting towards their lifetime gift exemption totals.

State Tax

If you happen to live in one of the eighteen states or the District of Columbia[2] that has its own estate or inheritance tax, generally with much lower exemptions than the federal level, your estate may be subject to state level taxation. That possibility may come as a rude surprise to grandparents who haven't recently consulted with their estate planning advisor. It may also make use of 529 plans to eliminate assets from your estate more appealing.

As you'd expect, these estate taxes vary considerably. State-to-state differences include the tax rates themselves, the levels at which point they become effective, and how they're implemented. Oregon and Massachusetts hold the record for the lowest exemption, or beyond what dollar amount estate taxes will be due. Both states have exemptions of $1 million, far below the federal $11.2 million exemption

[2] Ebeling, Ashlea, "Trusts in the Age of Trump: Time to Re-Engineer Your Estate Plan" Personal Finance, *Forbes,* February 13, 2018, *www.forbes.com.*

level. That lower exemption casts a wide net. In Oregon alone, there were 1,563 taxable estate tax returns in 2015.[3]

How your state implements their respective estate tax also bears scrutiny. A few states have "cliff taxes," whereby if your estate exceeds the exempt amount by even a single dollar, the tax isn't just on the dollar, but on your entire estate.[4] Ouch! Table 19.1 below illustrates estate exemption levels by state, or when estate taxes kick in.

Table 19.1
When estate taxes begin by state—2018[5]

STATE	ESTATE TAX EXEMPTION	MAXIMUM TAX RATE
Oregon	$1,000,000	16%
Massachusetts	1,000,000	16%
Rhode Island	1,540,000	16%
Washington	2,190,000	20%
Minnesota	2,400,000	16%
Connecticut	2,600,000	16%
Vermont	2,750,000	16%
Illinois	4,000,000	16%
Maryland	4,000,000	16%
New York	5,250,000	16%
Maine	11,200,000	12%
Hawaii	11,200,000	16%
District of Columbia	11,200,000	16%

[3] Ebeling, Ashlea, "Where Not to Die in 2018," Personal Finance, *Forbes*, December 21, 2017, *www.forbes.com*.

[4] Sheedy, Rachel L., "State Death Taxes Losing Life," Estate Planning, Kiplinger's Retirement Report, January 2017, *www.kiplinger.com*.

[5] "State Death Tax Chart," The American College of Trust and Estate Counsel, June 14, 2018, *www.actec.org*.

An additional six states employ an inheritance tax in which the recipients of a grandparent's generosity owe tax after the estate distribution. A common characteristic of inheritance taxes is that the further removed an inheritor is from the deceased (family member vs. a nonfamily member), the higher the tax rate. Table 19.2 shows the states and their maximum inheritance tax rates.

Table 19.2
Inheritance tax rates by state—2018[6]

STATE	MAXIMUM TAX RATE
Nebraska	18%
Kentucky	16%
New Jersey	16%
Pennsylvania	15%
Iowa	15%
Maryland	10%

Let's consider the case of a widowed grandmother with ten grandchildren residing in Washington State who passes away during 2018. After deducting all appropriate legal fees and paying off liabilities, her estate is valued at $5 million. She never did any estate planning because she thought the federal estate tax didn't start until a higher level. She had always wanted to provide a little extra help to her grandchildren, so she's leaving them each $75,000 in her will. That's great! But she hadn't realized Washington had an estate tax. A taxable estate of $5 million, after deducting the state's $2,193,000 exemption, will owe an estate tax of $361,000.

However, what if instead she had established a 529 plan for each grandchild and contributed five years' worth of her annual gift tax

---

[6] Walczak, Jared, "State Inheritance and Estate Taxes: Rates, Economic Implications and the Return of Interstate Competition," Washington DC: Tax Foundation, July 17, 2017.

exclusions, compressed or accelerated into that single year. Ten 529 contributions of $75,000 would have removed $750,000 from her taxable estate. This would have saved her estate—or in reality, her heirs—$112,500 in Washington State estate tax. And she would have had the joy and fulfillment of watching her grandchildren benefit from her generosity.

DEALING WITH UNCERTAINTY

A lot can happen in the intervening years or decades between the time you establish your grandchild's college savings plan and the time they'll need to actually withdraw those funds for their higher education aspirations. That's where the 529 plan's flexibility comes into play. The ability to change the educational beneficiary on the account, to open additional 529 accounts in multiple states, or to even retrieve funds if necessary enables grandparents to adjust to unforeseen changes.

For example, hidden amid the fanfare—or outrage—over the estate tax reduction within the Tax Cut and Jobs Act of 2017 is the fact that the tax exemption of $11.2 million returns to $5.5 million at the end of 2025. Additionally, as we all know, tax regulations, either at the federal or state level, can unexpectedly change depending on which political party holds sway. In the face of estate tax uncertainties years down the road, a 529 plan offers an effective long-term shelter from those unknowns.

WHAT HAPPENS TO MY 529 WHEN I PASS AWAY?

While probate and estate laws vary significantly from state to state, 529 plans generally escape the probate process entirely. Similar to life insurance, annuities, or retirement plan assets, 529 plan assets pass outside the probate process. They are considered stand-alone contractual agreements. Therefore, 529 plan holdings are not publically disclosed with your probate assets, and they are not passed on to your heirs per the terms of your will but by way of a specific 529 successor agreement.

When you establish your 529 college savings plan for the benefit of your grandchild, you'll be asked to assign a successor account owner. In the event of your death or incapacity while there are still funds in the account, the successor you name will become the account owner, with all the accompanying rights and restrictions. That individual can change the beneficiary or transfer account ownership, and they will be subject to taxes and penalties should withdrawals be used for non-qualified purposes.

If there is no legitimate successor for any number of reasons—your named successor has passed away, is incapable of discharging their duties, a successor was inadvertently never named—the student beneficiary of the account becomes the account owner. (The exception is if you've explicitly identified the alternative successor in your will.) If that student beneficiary is still a minor, not an unheard of occurrence for grandparents, a guardian must be appointed for the account. The 529 account may then become a Uniform Gifts to Minors Act (UGMA) custodial account until the student reaches the age of majority, at which point they can use the account for any purposes they wish, hopefully for education.

Looking at the potential complications of an account owner passing away without a named or living 529 plan successor, grandparents would do well to consider naming one of their grandchildren's parents, or another responsible family member of that generation, as the account successor. Grandparents might also consider passing the baton of 529 account ownership to others prior to it becoming an estate issue (i.e. while still alive) when their grandchild approaches the age of actually needing funds from the account.

CAVEATS

It's not all positive. There are several caveats to consider. First, unlike traditional assets that pass through the probate process, there is no step up in basis upon the death of the 529 account owner. Traditional assets inherited by your heirs have their cost basis, or taxable basis, increased to the value at the date of death. Assuming the assets have appreciated, this stepped-up basis will effectively eliminate significant capital gains if or when your heirs eventually sell those assets. Securities held inside a 529 plan, however, do not have their cost basis adjusted when the account's ownership is inherited by a successor. Obviously, this is a moot point if the funds are only withdrawn for qualified educational expenses as the earnings are tax-free. However, if the funds are used for nonqualified expenditures, the taxes and penalty would be based upon total earnings beyond the amount of funds contributed to the plan.

Second, if you've opted to super fund your grandchild's 529 savings plan (accelerating five years of contributions into one) and you unexpectedly pass away within that five-year period, a prorated portion of the contributions are considered part of the estate for tax purposes and subject to any applicable federal or state taxation.

Let's say that a grandparent in declining health has contributed five years of individual annual gift tax exclusions, which will total $75,000, to their grandchild's 529 college savings plan. If that grandparent should then pass away during the second year, the first two years of contributions, representing $30,000 would remain outside their estate. However, the contributions for the remaining three years, or $45,000, would be considered part of his or her estate and subject to possible taxation at the federal or state level.

There are countless variables to consider in crafting a customized estate plan, from complex tax and financial issues to emotionally charged family dynamics. While the unique features of a 529 plan make it a possible estate planning tool, you should always seek the counsel of a qualified estate planning professional when building your estate plan.

- Unique features enable 529 savings plans to be part of grandparents' estate plans
- 529 plans are typically immune from estate or inheritance taxes
- Don't forget to name a successor to your 529 saving's plan

Chapter 20

CREATING AN EDUCATIONAL DYNASTY

Centuries ago, Iroquois Native Americans developed a philosophy to guide the Iroquois Confederacy's most important decision-making. That philosophy encouraged leaders to weigh the impact of their decisions seven generations into the future. It has since been called the Seventh Generation Principle. Today, that forward-looking philosophy is praised for its wise stewardship in giving voice to unborn generations.

It is in that spirit of multigenerational wisdom that grandparents, with the financial means to do so, are encouraged to create an educational fund intended for perpetuity and designated to support their heirs' higher education. It's what I call the creation of an educational dynasty, and 529 savings plans provide the ideal administrative structure in which to build this educational legacy.

The word "dynasty" is most closely associated with families that periodically dominate politics, such as the Roosevelts, the Kennedys, or the Bushes. It's been used in the sports world to describe an unparalleled string of championships, such as UCLA basketball in the 1970s. The formal definition of a dynasty is "a powerful group or family that maintains its position for a considerable time."[1] Yet the term could apply equally to a succession of family members who have been able to maximize their educational opportunities.

Creating a formal tradition of assisting family members with post-secondary education will enable future generations to achieve their fullest potential—whether that education entails trade school, international studies, an associate's degree from community college, or a doctorate from a private university. Providing subsequent generations the opportunity to be all they're capable of being represents an invaluable legacy.

HOLDING 529 PLANS INSIDE A FAMILY TRUST

A legitimate concern in creating a long-term family education fund is the succession plan. After your passing, or after your ability or willingness to oversee the fund, how do you safely and responsibly pass that mantle on to the next generation? You could always select your most business-savvy and responsible child or in-law to become the 529 account owner. However, since a 529 account owner can personally withdraw funds, that possibility can raise a host of troubling scenarios. Your newly assigned account owner might unexpectedly pass away, with the family's education fund now in the hands of a spouse with very different plans for the money. An unexpected emergency might tempt the new account owner to "borrow" from the fund without a viable means for repayment. Or the new 529 account owner may find themselves in a no-win situation of determining which family members receive how much for schooling.

One solution to ensure the continuity of an education fund is to create a formal family trust that would then be the account owner of subsequent 529 plans. Section 529 of the U.S. tax code, the underlying foundation for all qualified tuition plans, states that any "person"

---

[1] Merriam-Webster Dictionary, *www.merriam-webster.com.*

can establish a 529 college savings plan. The Internal Revenue Service defines person to include an individual, trust, estate, partnership, or corporation.[2] States have the autonomy to determine their own 529 ownership guidelines. All states, with the lone exception of Iowa, embrace the expanded IRS definition of what constitutes a person, although some states accept trusts but not partnerships, or accept partnerships but not corporations, and so forth.

Conceptually, family trusts are created to protect and control the management and distribution of assets for future generations in the most tax-efficient manner possible. A trust can also provide privacy and protection against creditors. The terms and conditions of the trust are defined in an underlying document that is similar to a contract. The terms of the trust identify its underlying purpose, how funds should be managed, to whom money can ultimately be distributed, and who or what entity will serve as the trustee to ensure the provisions are followed.

The real significance in creating a family educational trust is that it can last for generations. And in determining the underlying terms of the trust, founders can formalize policies and procedures, such as which family members are eligible for educational support, as well as a formal succession plan to pass trustee oversight from one generation to the next. A policy can also address how funds should be distributed in the event the educational trust is no longer necessary.

TRUST LIFE SPAN

Unfortunately for farseeing grandparents wishing to embrace the Seventh Generation Principle, private trusts can't last forever. While statutes vary from state to state, typically a trust can last no longer than the life span of a person alive when the trust is created plus twenty-one years. So, if you create a family educational trust when

---

[2] Internal Revenue Code Section 7701(a)(14).

your grandson is first born, and he lives a long and fruitful life, the trust's maximum lifetime will probably be between 100 and 120 years. However, that encompasses quite a few generations. If the family educational trust is still in existence after all those years, aside from the countless heirs you've benefited, those then acting as trustees can determine the best means of restructuring the fund for the future.

AVOIDING THE TRUST TAXATION TRAP

A family education trust ensures long-term, multigenerational opportunities for higher education. Sounds great. But it also presents a potential tax trap. While capital gains, dividends, and interest within a family trust 529 savings plan are exempt from federal taxation, that same income occurring from non-529 funds inside a trust are subject to among the highest tax rates in the U.S. tax code. For example, in 2018, once long-term gains or qualified dividends surpass a mere $12,700, the trust pays the highest capital gain rate of 23.8 percent. Over the long term, that will take a huge bite from funds available for education.

As a result, families considering creation of an educational trust are advised to maintain as much of those funds as possible in tax-insulated 529 saving plans within the trust, as opposed to excess funds accumulating in the trust outside a 529 plan. Since the designated beneficiary or future student can easily be changed, it makes sense to hold as much of the funds as possible within 529 plans inside the trust.

CREATING THE TRUST

A family educational trust provides formal group oversight so your long-term legacy has greater continuity and sustainability. Creating such an entity, in conjunction with legal counsel, involves the following:

- Drafting the trust document detailing the terms and conditions to be followed.

- Considering key decision points:

  - Will the trust begin immediately or be established through your estate?

  - Will the trust be irrevocable or revocable? (tax implications)

  - How will family members qualify for educational support?

  - Which family members or what entity will serve as trustee? This is a particularly important decision. In the interest of oversight, it is recommended that more than one family member assume the trustee role or consider a corporate trustee.

  - If trustees are individuals, how will successor trustees be appointed?

  - In what circumstances would or should the trust be dissolved? (No more heirs? Free college tuition? Changes in tax regulations?) Who is authorized to unwind or dissolve the trust? In the event of trust dissolution, how will funds in the placeholder accounts be distributed? How will the funds in student 529 plans be distributed?

- Applying for the trust's Employer Identification Number (EIN), which is equivalent to an individual's social security number.

- Funding the trust, which can be accomplished with transferred securities, in addition to cash.

- Establishing 529 accounts for appropriate family members and surplus plans for possible placeholder beneficiaries. The trust now owns the 529 plans, not any individual.

ESTABLISHING SURPLUS 529 PLANS

To build educational funds for future generations, the trust is encouraged to create one or more surplus 529 plans beyond those established for current grandchildren. While the surplus plan or plans will be owned by the trust, the current beneficiary or beneficiaries would be a family member who has completed their postsecondary education. In essence, that beneficiary would be a placeholder for the 529 plan until the next generation arrives. At that point, the 529 account beneficiary can be changed to the new family member without adverse tax consequences.

REMARKABLE LONG, LONG-TERM COMPOUNDING

Early in my career as a financial advisor, I educated young couples about the power of long-term compounding with a hypothetical Christopher Columbus story. Upon landing in San Salvador in 1492, Columbus put $100 into two different investment products. The first investment paid 5 percent simple interest. It didn't pay interest on the interest, just on the original $100. Every year, the investment added another five dollars to Christopher's account. Today, 526 years later, Columbus's $100 investment would have grown to $2,730. Sounds pretty good.

However, he also invested $100 in an investment that paid compound interest, or 5 percent interest on the original investment plus interest on the interest he'd earned. How did the second $100 fare? Over 526 years, that investment would have grown to $13,316,252,198,088. That's over $13 trillion!

Granted, that's a slightly longer planning horizon than most of us are working with. But it dramatizes the amazing results gained from long-term tax-free compounding. It also hints at the potential in creating a multigenerational family educational fund.

Suppose a couple established a 529 plan for the benefit of their grandchild or grandchildren and, in funding the account, they contributed $100,000 more than they thought would be needed. If that $100,000 is left untouched and grows 6 percent per year, over the next two generations, or 48 years, it will have grown to $1,600,000 (doubling every twelve years). It takes vision and time, but seeds thoughtfully planted by grandparents or parents, can grow into the making of a true educational legacy.

ILLUSTRATION: THE JONES FAMILY EDUCATION/529 TRUST

The following is a conceptual illustration of how the hypothetical Jones family created an educational/529 Trust and by so doing were able to fund private ivy-league education for five grandchildren, ten great-grandchildren, and twenty great-great-grandchildren. The scenario below simplifies a host of factors for illustrative purposes.

Assumptions and simplifications to create the Jones Family illustration:

- Bill and Betty Jones implement this strategy in 2020 during which time their five grandchildren are all eight years old. (Remember this is just hypothetical.)

- All descendants will attend a private university for four years.

- The total four year cost of private college is $250,000 in 2020 and increases 4 percent per year thereafter.

- Funds invested in the 529 plans appreciate, after fees, at an annual rate of 7.2 percent, thereby doubling every ten years (simplifies our computations).

- All grandparent descendants have two children per couple.

- Maximum state 529 contributions increase with the rate of tuition inflation.

- Since funds can be freely transferred between 529 plans within the Trust, differences between descendant's educational costs can easily be accommodated.

So let's walk through our *highly* hypothetical scenario:

YEAR 2020: Bill and Betty Jones have five grandchildren – all eight years old. They establish an educational trust with guidance and drafting from their estate planning attorney. They have appointed their children as trustees of the Trust. The Trust is funded with $3 million. Immediately after funding the Trust, the trustees open and fund a 529 plan for each of the five grandchildren (beneficiaries) with $200,000 apiece. That totals $1 million, and the remaining $2 million is used to open four "placeholder" 529 accounts for the temporary benefit of the grandchildren's parents – although the Trust still "owns" the monies in these placeholder accounts. (Each of the four placeholder 529 accounts is seeded with $500,000, recognizing the state's per account maximum contribution limitations.)

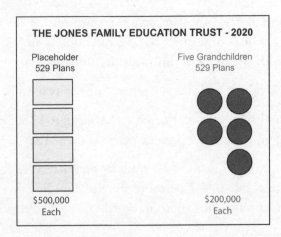

YEAR 2030: Bill's and Betty's five grandchildren are all entering college. Due to 7.2 percent annual tax-free appreciation, each of the grandchild's 529 account has grown to $400,000 which is fortunate since four years of elite private school now costs $370,000. The four 529 placeholder accounts have also doubled in value to a cumulative $4 million. In the subsequent four years the five individual grandchildren's 529 plans within the Trust are entirely spent down for college expenses – but all five grandchildren graduate!

YEAR 2040: Ten years later, all five grandchildren are married and each has two children. (Remember this is all hypothetical.) And in keeping with our simplification efforts, we'll assume the near impossible and that all ten great-grandchildren are born in 2040 – or perhaps each of the Jones off-spring simultaneously had a set of twins. The $4 million in the Jones Family Education/529 Trust placeholder accounts have now grown to $8 million. Upon the birth of those ten great-grandchildren, the trustees establish ten separate 529 savings plans, one for each great-grandchild, and each funded with $315,000 transferred from the placeholder accounts. At the end of 2040, the Jones Family Trust contains ten separate 529 plans, one for each great-grandchild, seeded with $315,000, and $4.85 million remaining in the four placeholder accounts within the Trust. As the generations age, the trusteeship is now passed to the next generation.

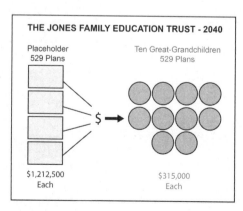

THE JONES FAMILY EDUCATION TRUST - 2040

Placeholder 529 Plans

Ten Great-Grandchildren 529 Plans

$ →

$1,212,500 Each

$315,000 Each

YEAR 2058: After nearly two more decades of tax-free growth, each of the ten great-grandchildren's 529 plan has grown to $1,100,000, which is fortunate since four years of elite private school now costs approximately $1,090,000 based on the ongoing 4 percent annual tuition inflation. The 529 placeholder accounts within the Trust have cumulatively grown to just under $17 million. In the subsequent four years the ten individual 529 plans within the Trust are entirely spent down for college expenses – but all ten great-grandchildren graduate!

YEAR 2070: This year the ten great-grandchildren have twenty great-great-grandchildren. The four placeholder accounts within the Jones Family Trust have grown to $39 million. During the year, the current trustees open twenty separate 529 plans, one for each great-great-grandchild, and each with $1,000,000 transferred from the four original placeholder accounts. At year end the Trust now has twenty 529 plans for the benefit of individual great-great grandchildren, with each containing $1,000,000. After funding the twenty separate accounts, the four placeholder accounts now hold a combined $19 million. As the generations age, the trusteeship is passed to the next generation.

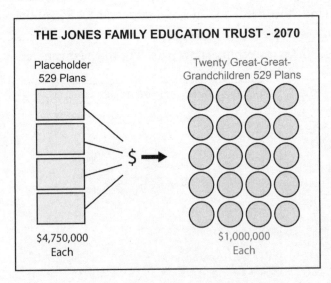

208

YEAR 2088: After another eighteen years of 7.2 percent tax-free growth, the Trust's four placeholder accounts cumulatively contain $66.4 million. Each of the twenty great-great-grandchild's separate 529 savings account has grown to $3.5 million, which is fortunate since four years of elite private school now costs $3.55 million after all those decades of 4 percent tuition inflation. In the subsequent four years the twenty individual 529 plans within the Trust are entirely spent down for college expenses – but all twenty great-great-grandchildren graduate!

We'll stop our hypothetical illustration here, sixty-eight years after Bill and Betty Jones first created the Jones Family Education/529 Trust. During the ensuing generations, Bill and Betty financed the college aspirations of five grandchildren, ten great-grandchildren, and twenty great-great grandchildren. Due to long-term compounding their original $4 million Trust contribution had grown by over $100 million in nominal dollars and because the gains all occurred within 529 plans, no taxes were paid by the Jones Family Trust along the way. Pretty remarkable!

SELECTING A 529 PLAN

Grandparents contemplating the creation of a multigenerational family education fund need to prioritize a different set of variables than the typical investor when selecting a 529 savings plan. Features that facilitate longevity are most important. The following 529 plan characteristics should be most heavily considered in plan selection:

- Trust ownership. Since the goal is for the fund to outlive any specific family member, a trust structure will be most beneficial. Make sure the state you select permits your preferred ownership structure.

- Account ownership transfers. If individuals, rather than the trust, will be the successive 529 account owners, it's important that ownership can be passed from one generation to the next. A few states do not permit the transfer of account ownership.

- No residency requirements. It's highly unlikely your grandchildren or great-grandchildren will all settle in the same state. Some states require the account owner or the beneficiary to be a state resident.

- Time limits. Fortunately, only a few states have maximum time limits on how long a 529 account can be in existence. Most have no time constraints.

- Investment returns and fees. Over several decades, modest reductions in fees and modest advantages in returns have a huge impact on the ultimate size of the education fund.

- Maximum asset contribution. Over multiple decades, this isn't quite as impactful as one would imagine, but a larger maximum contribution at the outset will certainly give the account a good head start.

By way of example, these priorities are evaluated in Table 20.1 below for the twelve states with the highest maximum contribution limits.

Table 20.1
529 plan state screening criteria
Family education trust

STATE	OWNERSHIP TRANSFER	TRUST OWNERSHIP	MAXIMUM CONTRIBUTION	ACCOUNT TIME LIMIT	RESIDENCY REQUIREMENT
New York	Yes	Yes	$520,000	None	No
Pennsylvania	Yes	Yes	511,758	None	Yes
District of Columbia	Yes	Yes	500,000	None	No
Louisiana	Only at death	Yes	500,000	None	Yes
Michigan	Yes	Yes	500,000	None	No
New Hampshire	Only at death	Yes	500,000	None	No
New Mexico	Yes	Yes	500,000	None	No
Virginia	Yes	Yes	500,000	30 Years	No
Alaska	Yes	Yes	475,000	None	No
California	Yes	Yes	475,000	None	No
Wisconsin	Yes	Yes	472,000	None	No
Ohio	Yes	Yes	462,000	None	No

MANAGING LONG-TERM INVESTMENTS

The establishment of a long-term, multigenerational family education fund, whether with stand-alone 529 plans or inside a trust, presents an investment opportunity not generally recommended for a single grandchild's 529 plan. Normally, it is recommended that as your grandchild gets closer and closer to college, the investments become less and less volatile, or there is a gradual reduction in stock holdings (known as the glide path).

However, if your family education goals include great-grandchildren and beyond, theoretically for perpetuity, funds should be invested akin to a university endowment. Endowments have no end point or target date. They can remain invested in growth-oriented portfolios, and you can rest easy in the knowledge that over the long-term, they'll experience far superior performance, while weathering year-to-year fluctuations or temporary market declines.

A FINAL WORD

An ancillary benefit in creating a long-term family educational fund may in fact be its most compelling aspect for some grandparents. Many families find that establishing a charitable-giving vehicle, such as a donor-advised fund or private foundation, is a means of creating family-wide participation and engagement, a unifying entity, or multigenerational touchstone.

In that same manner, a family educational fund can provide commonality, mutual purposefulness, a generational transfer of responsibilities, and a formal purpose for widely dispersed generations gathering together. It can become one more tradition that enables your family to maintain some of its unique identity for future generations. A family educational fund can do more than assist with post-secondary education.

No one knows what the future holds. Perhaps decades from now higher education will be free. Perhaps all education will be accomplished with a microchip implanted at birth. (When you consider virtually all the world's information is accessible via a handheld smartphone, the chip implant concept may not be so far-fetched.) Regardless of what lies ahead in terms of higher education, creation of a family education fund will help support your current and future heirs' highest aspirations. And should today's postsecondary education model radically change in unforeseen ways, those funds you wisely set aside decades earlier can be retrieved and repurposed for the benefit of your great-grandchildren and great-great-grandchildren. The advantages and features of 529 college savings plans, within a family trust, provide an excellent framework with which to start building a family educational legacy.

KEY CHAPTER TAKEAWAYS

- Grandparents have a unique opportunity to create a lasting family legacy of higher education

- 529 plans inside a trust provides a framework for smooth succession planning

- Investment management should account for the perpetuity of a family 529 savings plan trust

- Your wisdom in creating a family legacy of higher education will long be remembered and honored by future generations

Online 529 Plan Resources

Qualifying Educational Institutions

U.S. qualifying educational institutions:
https://fafsa.ed.gov/FAFSA/app/schoolSearch

International colleges qualifying for tax-free 529 plan distributions:
https://www.credible.com/blog/student-loans/international-schools-student-loans

How much will your Grandchild's College Really Cost?

CNN College Costs *http://money.cnn.com/tools/collegecost/collegecost.html*
College Affordability and Transparency Center *https://collegecost.ed.gov/catc/*
College Navigator: *https://nces.ed.gov/collegenavigator/*

In-Depth 529 Plan Information

Savingforcollege: Valuable resources including newsletters, cost of college calculators, and the ability to compare various 529 plans and other investment options. *www.savingforcollege.com*

College Savings Plans Network: The College Savings Plans Network is a national nonprofit association dedicated to making college more accessible and affordable for families. Its website provides detailed information about college savings plans and allows you to compare 529 plans from around the country. *www.collegesavings.org*

Financial Industry Regulatory Authority: Analyze 529 college savings plans fees and expenses.
http://apps.finra.org/investor_Information/Smart/529/Calc/529_Analyzer.asp

FINANCIAL AID

Federal Student Aid *https://studentaid.ed.gov/sa/*

U.S. Department of Education *https://fafsa.ed.gov/*

Schools using the CSS Profile scholarship and grant application form *https://profile.collegeboard.org/profile/ppi/participatinginstitutions.aspx*

FinAid *http://www.finaid.org/*

HOW FEES IMPACT YOUR 529 PLAN INVESTMENT PERFORMANCE

U.S. Securities and Exchange Commission
www.investor.gov/additional-resources/news-alerts/alerts-bulletins/updated-investor-bulletin-how-fees-expenses-affect

CALCULATORS

529 Plan Cost Comparison Calculator
www.aarpcollegesavings.com/tools-and-resources/tool-calculator.shtml

CalcXML
www.calcxml.com/calculators/529-college-savings-plan

Vanguard Savings Planner
https://vanguard.wealthmsi.com/csp.php

Bankrate
www.bankrate.com/calculators/savings/saving-for-college-calculator.aspx

College Savings Calculator
www.schwab.com/public/schwab/investing/retirement_and_planning/saving_for_college/college_savings_calculator

MISCELLANEOUS

Peterson's: Considered one of the comprehensive education resources on the Internet, Peterson's offers core products for college search and selection, test preparation, and financial aid. *http://www.petersons.com/*

The College Board: The College Board is a not-for-profit membership association whose mission is to connect students to college success and opportunity. Founded in 1900, the College Board is composed of more than 5,700 schools, colleges, universities, and other educational organizations. *https://www.collegeboard.org/*

Sources

Introduction

"10-Year College Progress Report: Fidelity Finds Record-High Number of Families Saving and Investing in 529 Plans," Fidelity Investments, August 25, 2016, www.fidelity.com.

"529 Report: An Exclusive Year-End Review of 529 Plan Activity," The College Savings Plans Network, March 2015, www.collegesavings.org.

Adam, Thomas, "From Public Good to Personal Pursuit: Historical Roots of the Student Debt Crisis," The Conversation, June 29, 2017, www.theconversation.com.

Boston Research Technologies, "10th Annual College Savings Indicator," Fidelity Investments, June 2016, www.fidelity.com.

Curley, Paul, "529 College Savings & Able, 529 Data Highlights: 4Q 2017," Strategic Insight, February 15, 2018, www.sionline.com.

"Despite All-Time High College Savings Rate, Families Underestimating Future College Costs," Fidelity Investments, October 12, 2017, www.fidelity.com.

"Distribution of Wealth in US by Age," Free By 50, September 6, 2012, www.freeby50.com.

Internal Revenue Tax Code – 529 Qualified Tuition Programs, www.uscode. house.gov.

Mukerji, S.N.; Scanlon, David G.; Szyliowicz, Joseph S.; Moumouni, Abdou; Graham, Hugh; Lawson, Robert F.; Education, *Encyclopedia Britannica*, www.britannica.com.

ORC International's CARAVAN Omnibus Surveys, "529 Plan Awareness Survey," Edward Jones, May 17, 2018, www.edwardjones.com.

Pentis, Andrew, "Survey: 44% of Parents Feel Guilty about Not Saving Enough for College," Student Loan Hero, May 15, 2018, www.studentloanhero.com.

Sallie Mae and Ipsos Public Affairs, *How America Pays for College–2016: Sallie Mae's National Study of College Students and Parents*, Newark, 2016, www.SallieMae.com.

Sallie Mae and Ipsos Public Affairs, *How America Pays for College–2017: Sallie Mae's National Study of College Students and Parents*, Newark, 2017, www.SallieMae.com.

CHAPTER 2 – THE GREATEST GIFT

Beebe, Marissa; Duncan, Stephen F.; "Importance of Grandparents to Their Grandchildren," Forever Families, School of Family Life, Brigham Young University, www.foreverfamilies.byu.edu.

Cohen, Daffnee, "Why We Need to Maintain Family Tradition," The Blog, Huffington Post, February 4, 2015, www.huffingtonpost.com.

Collier, Charles W., *Wealth in Families*, Boston: Harvard University, 2012.

Davidson, Adam, "Is College Tuition Really too High?" *The New York Times*, September 8, 2015.

DeTorres, Darrin, "The Importance of Higher Education in Today's Society," Darrinruns, February 23, 2012, www.darrinrunswordpress.com.

Doumbia, Kafoumba, "Why is Education so Important in our Life?" Commentary, EdLab August 18, 2013, www.edlab.tc.columbia.edu

Foleno, Tony; Immerwahr, John; *Great Expectations: How the Public and Parents—White, African-American and Hispanics—View Higher Education*, New York: The National Center for Public Policy and Higher Education, May 2000, www.highereducation.org.

Kane, Mary, "Gifting College to Your Grandchildren," Paying for College, Kiplinger's Retirement Report, April 6, 2018, www.kiplinger.com.

LaTour, Amee', "Top 4 Benefits of Higher Education Continuing After High School," Good Choices, Good Life, 2014, www.goodchoicesgoodlife.org.

Lewin, Tamar, "Study Finds Family Connections Give Big Advantages in College Admissions," Education, *The New York Time*s, January 8, 2011

Ma, Jennifer; Pender, Matea; Welch, Meredith; *Education Pays 2016—The Benefits of Education for Individuals and Society.* Boston: The College Board, 2016.

Powell, Mary Alice, "A Family Legacy of Education and Hope," Commentary, The Blade, November 13, 2016, www4.toledoblade.com.

O'Donnell, Martin, *College Savings Plans—Navigating the 529 College Savings Plans,* CreateSpace Independent Publishing Platform, December 7, 2010.

Schreur, Jerry; Schreur, Judy; "Grandparents as Role Models," Marriage, Focus on the Family, www.focusonthefamily.com.

Trafford, Abigail, "Grandparents Help Define Family Values," My Time, *The Washington Post*, March 1, 2005, www.washingtonpost.com.

Trostel, Philip, *It's Not Just the Money—The Benefits of College Education to Individuals and to Society.* Indianapolis: Lumina Foundation, 2015.

Williams, Joseph, "How Much is a College Degree Really Worth?" Take Part, June 8, 2016, www.takepart.com.

Chapter 3 – Background and History

Barron, James, "Michigan Governor to Urge College Tuition Guarantee," *The New York Times*, January 29, 1986.

Barron, James, "Education: Michigan Plan Guarantees College Tuition," *The New York Times*, December 30, 1986.

Berman, Russell, "Birth of a Tax Loophole," Politics, *The Atlantic*, March 16, 2015, www.theatlantic.com.

Brumbaugh, David, L., "The Taxpayer Relief Act of 1997: An Overview," Congressional Research Service, The Library of Congress, October 17, 1997.

Flynn, Kathryn, "The History of the 529 Plan," Savingforcollege, May 14, 2014, www.savingforcollege.com.

Gibson, Cary, "Obama's 529 Missteps, The President Erred When he Proposed Taxing College Savings Plans," *US News*, February 2, 2015, www.usnews.com.

Hannon, Simona; Moore, Kevin; Schmeiser, Max; Stefanescu, Irina; "Saving for College and Section 529 Plans," FEDS Notes, February 3, 2016, www.federalreserve.gov.

"History of 529 Plans," The College Savings Plan Network, www.college-savings.org.

Hurley, Joseph, *The Best Way to Save for College: A Complete Guide to 529 Plans*, SavingforCollege.com Publications, 2015.

Lane, Marc J., "New Tax Cut Makes Section 529 Plans Better than Ever," 2001 Lane Reports, March J. Lane Wealth Group, August 1, 2001, www.marcjlane.com.

McCullers, Madeline; Stafanescu, Irina; "Introducing Section 529 Plans into the U.S. Financial Accounts and Enhanced Financial Accounts," Fed Notes, December 18, 2015, www.federalreserve.gov.

"Pension Protection Act of 2006: Charitable Giving and Reform Measures Impacting Colleges and Universities," NACAU Notes, Volume 5, No. 1, December 19, 2006, www.untsystem.edu.

Pethokoukis, James, "A College Savings Plan with One Less Worry," Your Money, *The New York Times,* September 17, 2006, www.nytimes.com.

Stratford, Michael, "Politics of the 529 Plan," News, Inside Higher Ed, January 29, 2015, www.insidehighered.com.

CHAPTER 4 – THE RISING COST OF COLLEGE

Anschuetz, Nika, "Breaking the 4-Year Myth: Why Students are Taking Longer to Graduate," *USA Today College*, December 16, 2015, www.college.usatoday.com.

Bancalari, Kellie, "Private College Tuition is Rising Faster than Inflation… Again," College, *USA Today College*, June 9, 2017, www.college.usatoday.com.

Common College Completion Metrics Technical Guide, Indianapolis: Complete College America, March 28, 2017.

DeHahn, Patrick, "Bad News for Low-Income College Students in Trump 2017 Budget," *USA Today College*, March 16, 2017, www.college.usatoday.com.

Fay, Bill, "College Expenses: How Much Does a College Degree Really Cost?" 2018, www.debt.org.

Goldrick-Rab, Sara; McCluskey, Neal; "Should College Education Be Free?" *The Wall Street Journal*, March 20, 2018, www.wsj.com.

Helhoski, Anna, "How the Rise in Student Loan Rates will Affect Borrowers," NerdWallet, *USA Today College*, May 18, 2017, www.college.usatoday.com.

Hood, John, "Why College Costs are Rising," Foundation for Economic Education, November 1, 1988, www.fee.org.

Joslyn, Heather, "Giving to Colleges Up 6% in 2017," News and Analysis, *The Chronicle of Philanthropy*, February 6, 2018, www.philanthropy.com.

Kolodner, Meredith, "6 Reasons You May Not Graduate on Time (and What to Do about It)" Education, *The New York Times*, April 6, 2017.

McFarland, J., Hussar, B., de Brey, C., Snyder, T., Wang, X., Wilkinson-Flicker, S., Gebrekristos, S., Zhang, J., Rathbun, A., Barmer, A., Bullock Mann, F., and Hinz, S. (2017). *The Condition of Education 2017* (NCES 2017- 144). U.S. Department of Education. Washington, DC: National Center for Education Statistics.

Korte, Gregory, "The 62 Agencies and Programs Trump Wants to Eliminate," *USA Today*, March 17, 2017.

Reeves, Richard V.; Joo, Nathan; "A Tax Break for Dream Hoarders: What to do about 529 College Savings Plans," Washington DC: Brookings, June 29, 2017.

Rothman, Lily, "Putting the Rising Cost of College in Perspective," History-Education, *Time*, August 31, 2016, www.time.com.

Rubin, Elaine Griffin, "How Does Student Loan Interest Work," Edvisors, March 7, 2018, www.edvisors.com.

Seltzer, Rick, "Net Price Keeps Creeping Up," Inside Higher Ed, October 25, 2017, www.insidehighered.com.

Shapiro, D.; Dundar, A.; Wakhunga, P.K.; Yuan, X; Hwang, A; *Time to Degree: A National View of the Time Enrolled and Elapsed for Associate and Bachelor's Degree Earners,* Herndon, VA: National Student Clearinghouse Research Center, September 2016.

Sourmaids, Demetrius, "Rising Tuition Costs and the History of Student Loans," Student Debt Relief, January 3, 2018, www.Studentdebtrelief.us.

Ma, Jennifer, Sandy Baum, Matea Pender, and Meredith Welch (2017), *Trends in College Pricing 2017*, New York: The College Board.

U.S. Department of Education, *Digest of Education Statistics 2016*,

Washington DC: National Center for Education Statistics, (2016)

Williams, Joseph, "When It Comes to College Costs, Middle-Class Kids Are Still Screwed," Takepart, Politico, April 29, 2016, www.takepart.com.

Zurolo, Mark, "The Cost of Yale: A History," *Yale Alumni Magazine*, May/June 2015, www.yalealumnimagazine.com.

CHAPTER 5 – IS COLLEGE WORTH THE MONEY?

Carnevale, Anthony P.; Cheah, Ban; Hanson, Andrew R.; *The Economic Value of College Majors*, Washington DC: Georgetown University, Center on Education and the Workforce, McCourt School of Public Policy, 2015.

"Choice of College Major Influences Lifetime Earnings More than Simply Getting a Degree," EurekAlert! Science News, University of Kansas, September 16, 2015, www.eurekalert.org.

Dossani, Rafiq, "Is College Worth the Expense? Yes it is," Commentary, The Rand Blog, The Rand Corporation, May 22, 2017, www.rand.org.

"Going to the University is More Important than ever for Young People-But the Financial Returns are Falling," All Must Have Degrees, *The Economist*, February 3, 2018, www.economist.com

"Is College Worth Going into Debt For?" www.collegechoice.net.

"Is College Worth It?" Higher Education, *The Economist*, April 5, 2014, www.economist.com

Kaufman, Micha, "Is College Still Worth it?" Entrepreneurs, *Forbes,* March 20, 2015. www.forbes.com.

Kim, C; Tamborini, C. R.; Sakamoto A; "Field of Study in College and Lifetime Earnings in the United States," *Sociology of Education*, September 2015.

Kroeger, Theresa; Cooke, Tanyell; Gould, Elise; *The Class of 2016: The Labor Market is Still Not Ideal for Young Graduates,* Washington DC: Economic Policy Institute, April 21, 2016, www.epi.org.

Ma, Jennifer; Pender, Matea; Welch, Meredith; *Education Pays 2016: The Benefits of Higher Education for Individuals and Society*, New York: The College Board, 2016.

Mitchell, Josh; Belkin, Douglas; "Americans Losing Faith in College Degrees," *The Wall Street Journal*, September 7, 2017.

Moss, Wes, "Why a College Degree is Still Worth It," Life Stages, Financial Planning, The Balance, March 6, 2018, www.thebalance.com.

"Special Report: Is College Still Worth the Debt?" www.collegechoice.net.

Unemployment Rates and Earnings by Educational Attainment-2016, Washington DC: U.S. Bureau of Labor Statistics, Current Population Survey, October 24, 2017.

Weissman, Shoshana; Dieterle, C. Jarrett; "Why Do You Need a College Degree to Give Diet Advice?" Commentary, *The Wall Street Journal*, January 31, 2018, www.wsj.com.

Zorthian, Julia, "Americans are Divided on Whether College Degrees Are Worth it," *Fortune*, September 7, 2017, www.fortune.com.

Chapter 6 – Insulating Your Grandchildren from Financial Zombies

"A Look at the Shocking Student Loan Debt Statistics for 2018," Student Loan Hero, January 2, 2018, www.studentloanhero.com.

Baum, Sandy; Ma, Jennifer; Pender, Matea; Welch, Meredith; *Trends in Student Aid 2017*, New York: The College Board, 2017.

Boushey, Heather, *Student Debt: Bigger and Bigger*, Washington, D.C., Center for Economic and Policy Research, September 2005.

Brown, Meta; Haughwout, Andrew; Lee, Danghoon; Scally, Joelle; Van der Klaauw, Wilbert; *Looking at Student Loan Defaults through a Larger Window*, Federal Reserve Bank of New York, Liberty Street Economics, www.libertystreeteconomics.newyorkfed.org, February 19, 2015.

Carroll, C. Dennis; Choy, Susan P.: Li, Xiaojie; *Dealing with Debt: 1992-93 Bachelor's Degree Recipients 10 Years Later*, U.S. Department of Education, Washington, DC: National Center for Educational Statistics, June 2006.

Corkery, Michael; Cowley, Stacy; "Household Debt Makes a Comeback in the U.S.," DealBook, *The New York Times,* May 17, 2017, www.nytimes.com.

Delisle, Jason, *The Graduate Student Debt Review – The State of Graduate Student Borrowing* New America Education Policy, March 25, 2014, www.newamerica.org.

DeSilver, Drew, "In Time for Graduation Season, a Look at Student Debt," FactTank – News in the Numbers, Pew Research Center, May 13, 2017, www.pewresearch.org.

DiGangi, Christine, "The Average Student Loan Debt in Every State," Money, *USA Today*, April 28, 2017.

DiGangi, Christine, "The Class of 2016 Will Graduate With an Average of $37,172 in Debt," College Planning, Fox Business, May 6, 2016, www.foxbusiness.com.

Douglas-Gabriel, Danielle, "College Costs Rising Faster than Financial Aid, Report Says," Grade Point, *The Washington Post*, October 26, 2016, www.washingtonpost.com.

Editorial, "Student Debt's Grip on the Economy," *The New York Times*, May 20, 2017, www.nytimes.com.

Ferek, Kathy Stech, "Judges Wouldn't Consider Forgiving Student Loans-Until Now," *The Wall Street Journal*, June 14, 2018, www.wsj.com.

Friedman, Zack, "Can Student Loans Now Be Discharged in Bankruptcy?" *Forbes*, June 18, 2018, www.forbes.com.

Gillers, Heather; Scism, Leslie; Tergesen, Anne; "A Generation of Americans is Entering Old Age the Least Prepared in Decades," *The Wall Street Journal*, June 22, 2018, www.wsj.com

Ginder, Scott A.; Kelly-Reid, Janice E.; Mann, Farrah B.; *2015–2016 Integrated Postsecondary Education Data System Methodology Report*, Washington,

DC: U.S. Department of Education, National Center for Education Statistics, September 2016.

Holland, Kelley, "The High Economic and Social Costs of Student Loan Debt," Debt by Degree, CNBC, June 15, 2015, www.cnbc.com.

"Household Debt and Credit Report, 1st Quarter 2018," Center for Microeconomic Data, New York: Federal Reserve Bank of New York, June 2018.

Howard, Patrick J., *The Department's Communication Regarding the Costs of Income-Driven Repayment Plans and Loan Forgiveness Programs,* Washington, D.C.: U.S. Department of Education, Office of Inspector General, January 31, 2018.

Insler, Shannon, "5 Ways Student Loans Can Help—or Hurt—Your Credit," Student Loan Hero, February 28, 2018, www.studentloanhero.com.

Insler, Shannon, "Millennials with Student Loans See 35% Decline in Homeownership," Student Loan Hero, July 14, 2017, www.studentloanhero.com.

Insler, Shannon, "Student Loan Default: Everything You Need to Know," Student Loan Hero, August 4, 2017, www.studentloanhero.com.

Izzo, Phil, "Number of the Week: Class of 2013, Most Indebted Ever," Real Time Economics, *The Wall Street Journal,* May 18, 2013, www.blogs.wsj.com.

Looney, Adams; Yannelis, Constantine; *A Crisis in Student Loans? How Changes in the Characteristics of Borrowers and in the Institutions They Attended Contributed to Rising Loan Defaults,* Washington, D.C.: Brookings, Fall 2015, www.brookings.edu.

Loudenback, Tanza, "Middle-class Americans Made More Money Last Year than Ever Before," Business Insider, September 12, 2017, www.businessinsider.com.

Marquit, Miranda, "Here's Why 5 Million Borrowers Are Defaulting on Student Loans," Student Loan Hero, December 15, 2017, www.studentloanhero.com

Marquit, Miranda, "Is the Student Loan Bubble Ready to Pop? One Expert Weighs In," Student Loan Hero, June 28, 2017, www.studentloanhero.com.

Mezza, Alvaro A.; Ringo, Daniel R.; Sherland, Shane M.; Sommer, Kamila, *On the Effect of Student Loans on Access to Homeownership*, Washington, D.C., Board of Governors of the Federal Reserve System, Finance and Economics Discussion Series, 2016.

Mitchell, Josh, "Federal Student-Loan Program Looks Set to Start Losing Money," Education, *The Wall Street Journal*, February 2, 2018, www.wsj.com.

Mitchell, Josh, "Nearly 5 Million Americans in Default on Student Loans," Education, *The Wall Street Journal*, December 13, 2017, www.wsj.com.

Mitchell, Josh, "The Rise of the Jumbo Student Loan Raises a Red Flag," Education, *The Wall Street Journal*, February 16, 2018, www.wsj.com.

"New Survey: What Do Young Workers Think About Student Loan Repayment Benefits?" Millennial Personal Finance, https://bit.ly/2wvMN8m, October 24, 2017.

"The Burden of Student Loan Debt Could Hurt Future Homeowners," Finance, *Fortune*, April 3, 2017, www.fortune.com.

Schoenberger, Chana R., "College-Aid Offers Aren't Set in Stone," Saving for College, *The Wall Street Journal*, April 9, 2018, www.wsj.com.

Scott-Clayton, Judith, *The Looming Student Loan Default Crisis Is Worse than We Thought*, Washington, DC: Brookings, January 11, 2018, www.brookings.edu.

"State of Student Debt in the U.S. – Part 2," Center for Online Education, www.onlinecolleges.net.

Umpierrez, Amanda, "Workers Will Sacrifice Benefits for Student Loan Repayment Options," Data and Research, *Plan Sponsor*, November 13, 2017, www.plansponsor.com.

U.S. Bureau of the Census, Current Population Reports, Series P-60, No. 174, *Money Income of Households, Families and Persons in the United States: 1990*, U.S. Government Printing Office, Washington, D.C., 1991.

Velez, Erin Dunlop; Woo, Jennie H.; RTI International; *The Debt Burden of Bachelor's Degree Recipients,* U.S. Department of Education, Washington, DC: National Center for Education Statistics, April 2017.

Walsemann, Katrina M.; Gee, Gilbert C.; Gentile, Danielle; "Sick of Our Loans: Student Borrowing and the Mental Health of Young Adults in the U.S.," *Social Science & Medicine,* Volume 124, January 2015.

Chapter 8 – Maximizing Tax Incentives

Backman, Maurie, "Can I Claim the Lifetime Learning Credit?" The Motley Fool, February 15, 2017, www.fool.com.

"Education Credits (American Opportunity and Lifetime Learning Credits) – Form 8863," Department of the Treasury, Internal Revenue Service, 2017, www.irs.gov.

Frankel, Matthew, "Your 2108 Guide to College Tuition Breaks – Here are the Details about the Three Ways Tuition Could Translate into Savings in 2018," The Motley Fool, March 17, 2018, www.fool.com.

Marks Jarvis, Gail, "Column: Student Tax Breaks Survive the Tax Bill, Make the Most of Them," Money, Reuters, December 20, 2017, www.reuters.com.

Marquit, Miranda, "The American Opportunity Credit 2017–2018: How to Save Thousands on College," Student Loan Hero, October 18, 2017, www.studentloanhero.com.

Measom, Cynthia, "Here's Who Can Claim the American Opportunity Credit," Go Banking Rates, December 23, 2017, www.gobankingrates.com.

Monroe, Rosa, "Do You Qualify for Lifetime Learning Credit?" Taxes, Bankrate, November 14, 2017, www.bankrate.com.

Nichols, Nancy B.; Ferguson, Susan Q.; VanDenburgh, William M.; "Dependency Exemption Issues for College Students," The Tax Adviser, July 31, 2010, www.thetaxadviser.com.

Perez, William, "Learn about the Lifetime Learning Credit," Taxes, The Balance, February 20, 2018, www.thebalance.com.

Saunders, Laura, "The New Tax Law: Standard Deduction and Personal Exemption," Wealth Management, *The Wall Street Journal*, February 13, 2018, www.wsj.com.

"Tax Benefits for Education – Publication 970, "Department of the Treasury, Internal Revenue Service, 2017, www.irs.gov.

"Tuition and Fees Deduction Instructions – Form 8917," Department of the Treasury, Internal Revenue Service, 2017, www.irs.gov.

CHAPTER 9 – FAMILY ISSUES

"Fifth Annual Survey – Discover Student Loans," Rasmussen Reports, Discover Financial Services, May 9, 2016, www.discover.com.

Kane, Libby, "Should You Give Your Kids Their Inheritance Before You Die?" LearnVest, The Week, August 21, 2013, www.theweek.com.

Meeker, Dr. Meg, "Grandparent Giving: Unspoken Secrets You Must Know Before Giving Gifts," Dave Ramsey, www.daveramsey.com.

"Moms and Dads Attaching More Strings to Paying for College," Discover Financial Services, July 21, 2014, www.aol.com.

"More Students Expected to Help Pay for College as Parents Become Less Worried about Costs," Business Wire, Discover Student Loans, May 9, 2016, www.businesswire.com.

Spragins, Ellyn, "When Parental Gifts Come with Strings Attached," Love & Money, *The New York Times*, December 7, 2003, www.nytimes.com.

Van Vuuren, Erin, "Back Off, Grandma! Dealing with Pushy Parents and In-Laws," The Bump, December 12, 2014, www.thebump.com.

CHAPTER 10 – CONTRIBUTION STRATEGIES

Clark, Ken, "What are the Benefits of Indiana's 529 Savings Plans?" Paying for College, The Balance, April 4, 2017, www.thebalance.com.

Garber, Julie, "IRS Form 709 Definition and Description," Estate Planning, The Balance, April 8, 2018, www.thebalance.com.

Gobel, Reyna, "Watch Out for Lifetime Limits on College Savings Plans," *US News & World Report*, November 27, 2013, www.usnews.com.

Huang, Chye-Ching, "Doubling Estate Tax Exemption Would Give Windfall to Heirs of Wealthiest Estates," Center on Budget and Policy Priorities, November 9, 2017, www.cbpp.org.

"Instructions for Form 709–2017," Internal Revenue Service, Department of the Treasury.

Lankford, Kimberly, "How to Transfer Money Between 529 College-Savings Accounts," Ask Kim, *Kiplinger*, June 28, 2016, www.kiplinger.com.

Pritchard, Justin, "529 Contribution Limits," Paying for College, The Balance, March 17, 2018, www.thebalance.com.

"United States Gift (and Generation-Skipping) Tax Return–2017," Internal Revenue Service, Department of the Treasury.

CHAPTER 11 – INVESTING 529 PLAN ASSETS

Acheson, Leo, *Morningstar Names Best College Savings Plans for 2017*, Chicago: Morningstar, October 24, 2017, www.morningstar.com.

Acheson, Leo; Holt, Jeff; Yang, Janet; *529 College-Savings Plan Landscape*, Chicago: Morningstar, May 26, 2016, www.morningstar.com.

Bennett, David A.; Boyle, Patricia A.; Gamble, Keith Jacks; Yu, Lei; *How Does Aging Affect Financial Decision Making?* Boston: Center for Retirement Research at Boston College, January, 2015.

Boswell, Brian, "How to Select Investments in a 529 Plan," Savingforcollege. com, July 15, 2016, www.savingforcollege.com.

Carlson, Josh; Liu, Laura; Lutton, Laura Pavlenko; Yang, Janet; *2011 529 College Savings Plans Research Paper and Industry Survey*, Chicago: Morningstar Fund Research, October 2011.

Carrns, Ann, "How to Manage a 529 Plan for Your Child's Education," *The New York Times*, February 2, 2017, www.nytimes.com.

Chang, C. Edward; Krueger, Thomas; "529 Plan Investment Advice: Focusing on Equity Concentration and Fees," *Journal of Financial Planning* 2018, 31 (6): 34–43.

Hurley, Joseph, "Understanding 529 Investment Options," Savingforcollege. com, December 13, 2016, www.savingforcollege.com.

Lutton, Laura Pavlenko; Liu, Laura; *2013 529 College Savings Plans Industry Survey*, Chicago: Morningstar, April 25, 2013, www.morningstar.com.

Ping, Jonathan, "Benjamin Franklin and Compound Interest: Money makes money. And the money that money makes, makes money," My Money Blog, March 15, 2015, www.mymoneyblog.com.

Poirier, Ryan; Soe, Aye M.; "SPIVA® U.S. Scorecard, S&P Dow Jones Indices, Mid-year 2016 Report." www.us.spindices.com.

U.S. Securities and Exchange Commission, *An Introduction to 529 Plans,* Investor Publications, December 4, 2017, www.sec.gov.

Williams, Andrea, "Consider these 529 Savings Plan Investment Options," Education, *U.S. News & World Report*, September 24, 2015, www.usnews.com.

Chapter 12 – Opening the Kindergarten Floodgates?

"2018 Tax Information for Wisconsin Account Owners," Wisconsin 529 College Savings Program, 2018, www.529.wi.gov.

Berical, Matt, "Final Tax Bill Expands 529 College Savings Plans at a Cost to Public Schools," Fatherly, December 20, 2017, www.fatherly.com.

Bier, Jerilyn Klein, "The Latest College Scene," *Financial Advisor*, March 1, 2018, www.fa-mag.com.

Brown, Lisa, "2018 Could be Grandparents' Year to Pump $150,000 into 529 Plans," *Kiplinger*, January 25, 2018, www.kiplinger.com.

Burke, Lindsey; Butcher, Jonathan; *Improved and Expanded 529 Savings Plans Create More Opportunities for Families*, Washington DC: The Heritage Foundation, December 27, 2017, www.heritage.edu.

Crunden, E. A., "Senate Republicans are Essentially Defunding Public Schools to Pay for Private Ones," Thinking Progress, December 2, 2017, www.thinkprogress.org.

Curley, Paul, "529 Product Development Implications of Tax Reform," Strategic Insight, January 29, 2018, www.strategic-i.com.

Flynn, Kathryn, "529 Funding Strategies for K-12 Private School Tuition," Savingforcollege.com, February 8, 2018, www.savingforcollege.com.

Flynn, Kathryn, "Don't count on a 529 State Tax Break for K-12 Tuition," Savingforcollege.com, January 10, 2018, www.savingforcollege.com.

Flynn, Kathryn, "What Tax Reform Really Means for 529 Plans," *Forbes*, December 15, 2017, www.forbes.com.

Hackman, Michelle, "States Worry You May Claim 529 Tax Exemption for K-12 School Tuition," Education, *The Wall Street Journal*, February 16, 2018.

Hammel, Paul, "State Treasurer Seeks to Postpone Tax Benefit for Private K-12 Tuition," *Omaha World-Herald*, December 30, 2017.

Hess, Frederick M., "Congress' Expansion of 529 Plans is Modest but Appropriate," AEI Ideas, American Enterprise Institute Ideas, January 2, 2018, www.aei.org.

Jarvis, Gail Marks, "Using 529 Funds to Pay for Private School? Check New Rules," Reuters, January 24, 2018, www.reuters.com.

Leamy, Elisabeth, "You can now use a 529 to pay for K-12 tuition—so should you?" On Parenting, *The Washington Post,* February 28, 2018, www.washingtonpost.com.

Lieber, Ron, "The Private School Tax Break in the Middle-Class Tax Bill," *The New York Times,* November 8, 2017, www.nytimes.com.

Lieber, Ron, "Yes, You Really Can Pay for Private School with 529 Plans Now," *The New York Times,* December 21, 2017, www.nytimes.com.

Malkus, Nat, "How the Republican Tax Plan Uses School Savings to Hurt States," *The New York Times,* December 19, 2017, www.nytimes.com.

Mulhere, Kaitlin, "The Tax Law's Biggest Education Change is on Hold in Several States," *Yahoo Finance*, January 9, 2018, www.finance.yahoo.com.

Phillips, Jeffrey, "How the New Tax Law Changed the 529 Plan Game Board", Think Advisor, March 31, 2018, www.thinkadvisor.com.

Ryan, Casey, "Mike Pence Helps Pass Cruz Amendment Expanding 529 Plans," Education, The Daily Signal, December 7, 2017, www.dailysignal.com.

Schoenberger, Chana R., "What to Consider Before Using a 529 to Pay for K-12 Costs," Saving for College, *The Wall Street Journal,* February 4, 2018, www.wsj.com.

Schoenberger, Chana R., "How a Grandparent's '529' Account Affects Financial Aid," *The Wall Street Journal*, August 3, 2018, www.wsj.com.

Sheldon, Steven, "K-12: A New 529 Planning Opportunity?" *Financial Advisor*, January 23, 2018, www.fa-mag.com.

Waddell, Melanie, "Kentucky to Allow 529 Plan Savers to Use Funds for K-12 Tuition, ThinkAdvisor, July 9, 2018, www.thinkadvisor.com.

CHAPTER 13 – FINANCIAL AID AND 529 PLANS

"A Recent Rule Change can Make a 529 Plan Even Better for You and Your Family," Vanguard, July 25, 2016, www.investornews.vanguard.com.

Baum, Sandy; Ma, Jennifer; Pender, Matea; Welch, Meredith; (2017), *Trends in Student Aid 2017*, New York: The College Board.

Belkin, Douglas, "In Many States, Students at Public Universities Foot Biggest Part of the Bill," Education, *The Wall Street Journal*, March 29, 2018, www.wsj.com.

"Can I Move Money from Another 529 Plan to this 529 Plan?" Wealthfront, May 21, 2018, www.support.wealthfront.com.

Cheng, Marguerita M., "How Can I Move My Funds from One 529 Plan to Another without Incurring Taxes?" Savingforcollege.com, April 21, 2015, www.savingforcollege.com.

Dagher, Veronica, "Mistakes to Avoid When Filling Out the CSS Profile for College Financial Aid," Wealth Management, *The Wall Street Journal*, September 10, 2017, www.wsj.com.

Douglas-Gabriel, Danielle, "How your Family Finances Factor into Financial Aid Calculations," *The Washington Post*, January 14, 2015, www.washingtonpost.com.

"Family Incorrectly Reported 529 Plan as a Student Asset on the FAFSA," Fastweb, August 31, 2017, www.fastweb.com.

Federal Student Aid, Office of the U.S. Department of Education, www.fafsa.ed.gov.

Flynn, Kathryn, "Yes, your 529 Plan will Affect Financial Aid," Savingforcollege.com, March 14, 2018, www.savingforcollege.com.

"How Do Grandparent-Owned 529 College Savings Plans Affect Financial Aid Eligibility?" Fastweb, August 31, 2017, www.fastweb.com.

"How Student and Parent Income Affect Your Financial Aid", College Data, www.collegedata.com.

Hurley, Joseph, "FAFSA Changes Make Grandparent 529 Plans Even Better," The Little Black Book of Billionaire Secrets, *Forbes*, September 17, 2015, www.forbes.com.

Kitces, Michael, "Grandparent 529 Plans and Gifting Appreciated Assets While Qualifying for FAFSA Financial Aid," May 11, 2016, www.kitces.com.

Levy, David, "CSS Financial Aid Profile," Edvisors, www.edvisors.com.

McFarland, J.; Hussar, B.; de Brey, C.; Snyder, T.; Wang, X.; Wilkinson-Flicker, S.; Gebrekristos, S.; Zhang, J.; Rathbun, A.; Barmer, A.; Bullock Mann, F.; Hinz, S; Washington DC: *The Condition of Education 2017*, National Center for Education Statistics.

Nykiel, Teddy, "CSS Profile: Everything You Need to Know in 2018-2019," Nerdwallet, October 30, 2017, www.nerdwallet.com.

Onink, Troy, "2017 Guide to College Financial Aid - The FAFSA and CSS Profile," The Little Black Book of Billionaire Secrets, *Forbes*, January 8, 2017, www.forbes.com.

Onink, Troy, "The Truth About Grandparent-Owned 529 College Savings Plans and College Aid," The Little Black Book of Billionaire Secrets, *Forbes*, May 31, 2015, www.forbes.com.

"The President's Plan for Early Financial Aid: Improving College Choice and Helping Americans Pay for College," Office of the Press Secretary, The White House, September 13, 2015, www.obamawhitehouse.archives.gov.

Schoenberger, Chana R., "Saving for College," *The Wall Street Journal*, March 5, 2018, www.wsj.com.

"Section 539 College Savings Plan Loophole," FinAid, www.finaid.org.

Stalter, Kate, "Grandparents: Don't Make a 529 Plan Mistake," *US News & World Report*, September 8, 2015, www.money.usnews.com.

"Fill Out the FAFSA?" Sallie Mae, www.salliemae.com.

"Which 529 College Savings Plans are Reported on the FAFSA?" Fastweb, August 24, 20178, www.fastweb.com.

CHAPTER 14 – DISTRIBUTION AND WITHDRAWAL STRATEGIES

"Higher Education Expenses that Qualify for 529 College Savings Plans," Personal Finance, Dummies, www.dummies.com.

"How to Spend from a 529 College Plan," Fidelity Viewpoints, January 24, 2018, www.fidelity.com.

Hurley, Joseph, "Don't Make These Mistakes When Reporting 529 Plan Withdrawals," The Little Book of Billionaire Secrets, *Forbes*, February 4, 2016, www.forbes.com.

Hurley, Joseph, "529 Rules Apply to Many Foreign Schools," Savingforcollege.com, December 31, 2017, www.savingforcollege.com.

Hurley, Joseph, *The Best Way to Save for College: A Complete Guide to 529 Plans*, Savingforcollege.com Publications, 2015.

Martin, Ray, "The Tricky Timing of 529 Savings Account Withdrawals," MoneyWatch, May 18, 2016, www.cbsnews.com.

McKinley, Kevin, "The Pitfalls and Perils of 529 Withdrawals," College Planning, Wealth Management, March 25, 2015, www.wealthmanagement.com.

Mert, Martha Kortiak, "What You can Pay for with a 529 Plan," Savingforcollege.com, May 17, 2018, www.savingforcollege.com.

Schultz, B. L., "529 Plan Withdrawals – Rules and Guidelines," The Money Skinny, February 27, 2017, www.themoneyskinny.com.

Schoenberger, Chana R., "Can I Use '529' College Money Overseas?" Saving for College, *The Wall Street Journal*, January 8, 2017, www.wsj.com.

"Supplement to New York's 529 College Savings Program Direct Plan Disclosure Booklet and Tuition Savings Agreement," New York's 529 College Savings Program, 2017, www.docucu-archive.com.

"What is the penalty for Early Withdrawal from 529 Plans?" The Motely Fool's Knowledge Center, February 9, 2018, www.fool.com.

Williams, Andrea, "4 Common Questions about Spending 529 College Savings Funds," *US News & World Report*, June 17, 2015, www.usnews.com.

Ziff, Deborah, "4 Surprising Places to Use 529 Plan College Savings," *US News & World Report*, April 6, 2016, www.usnews.com.

Chapter 15 – "My Grandchild has a Disability"

"529 ABLE Accounts," Savingforcollege.com, www.savingforcollege.com.

"Able Accounts: 10 Things You Should Know," ABLE National Resource Center, www.ablenrc.org.

"ABLE Accounts – (529 A Savings Plans)" Saving for College, FINRA, 2018, www.finra.org.

Adcox, Susan, "Grandparenting Special Needs Children – Coping With Challenges is a Family Affair," *The Spruce*, February 17, 2017, www.thespruce.com.

Diament, Michelle, "Tax Law Brings ABLE Changes, Future Worries," Disability Scoop, January 9, 2018, www.disabilityscoop.com.

Ebeling, Ashlea, "Fidelity Launches 529-ABLE Accounts, Tax-Free Savings for Disability Expenses," The Little Black Book of Billionaire Secrets, *Forbes*, May 10, 2017, www.forbes.com.

Flynn, Kathryn, "The ABLE Act and what it means for your 529 Plan," Savingforcollege.com, December 23, 2014, www.savingforcollege.com.

Kitces, Michael, "Will 529A ABLE Accounts Replace the Need for Disabled Beneficiary Special Needs Trusts?" MichaelKitces.com, March 4, 2015, www.kitces.com.

"New Tax Law Makes Changes to ABLE Accounts," Special Needs Answers, Academy of Specials Needs Planners, December 29, 2017, www.specialneedsanswers.com.

Saunders, Laura, "The New Tax Law: 529 Education Savings Accounts," Wealth Management, *The Wall Street Journal*, February 14, 2018, www.wsj.com.

Tay, Daniel, "Maryland Prohibits Medicaid Clawbacks from ABLE Programs," Law360, May, 9, 2018, www.Law360.com.

Turner, Scott Alan, "529 ABLE Plans: Saving for Children with Disabilities," December 19, 2016, www.scottalanturner.com.

"When You Have a Special Needs Grandchild," AARP, American Grandparents Association, www.Grandparents.com.

CHAPTER 16 – PREPAID TUITION PLAN OVERVIEW

"529 Prepaid Tuition Plans," Financial Industry Regulation Authority, www.finra.org.

Bernardo, Richie, "Prepaid Tuition Plans, Pros, Cons, How They Work & More," Wallethub, August 5, 2015, www.wallethub.com.

Couch, Christina, "Pros and Cons of Prepaid Tuition Plans," Student Loans, Bankrate, June 3, 2011, www.bankrate.com.

Flynn, Kathryn, "Prepaid College Savings Plans: Here's What You Need to Know," Savingforcollege.com, December 12, 2017, www.savingforcollege.com.

Gobel, Reyna, "Avoid These Common Prepaid Tuition Plan Mistakes," *US News & World Report*, July 24, 2013, www.usnews.com.

Hemelt, Steven A.; Marcotte, Dave E.; *The Changing Landscape of Tuition and Enrollment in American Public Higher Education*, New York: The Russell Sage Foundation, Journal of the Social Sciences, Volume 2, Number 1, April 2016.

Hurley, Joseph; McBride, Greg; "Does Your State's Prepaid Tuition Plan Make Sense," Savingforcollege.com, January 8, 2010, www.savingforcollege.com.

Kantrowitz, Mark, "List of State Prepaid Tuition Plans," Cappex, June 28, 2017, www.cappex.com.

Malagon, Elvia, "State Prepaid Tuition Program Comes to a Halt Again," *Chicago Tribune*, December 6, 2017, www.chicagotribune.com.

Maryland529, "2017/2018 Maryland Prepaid College Trust–Disclosure Statement and Enrollment Form," 2017, www.maryland529.com.

"Prepaid Tuition Plans–Listed by State," Edvisors, 2017, www.edvisors.com.

"Section 529 Plans," FinAid, www.finaid.org.

Virginia Prepaid529, "Program Description," December 1, 2017, www.virginia529.com.

"Washington State Guaranteed Education Tuition Program," 2018, www.get.wa.gov.

CHAPTER 17 – ALTERNATIVE INVESTMENTS FOR COLLEGE

2017 - How America Pays for College–Sallie Mae's 10th National Study of College Students and Parents, Newark: Sallie Mae, Washington DC: Ipsos Public Affairs, 2017.

"2018 Kiddie Tax: New Rules Means New Strategies," 4Thought Blog, Concannon Miller, February 8, 2018, www.blog.concannonmiller.com.

Aruldoss, Robert G., "Saving for College: Coverdell Education Savings Accounts," Personal Finance & Planning, Schwab Investment Company, April 16, 2018, www.schwab.com.

Baldwin, William, "Paying for College: UTMA and UGMA Accounts," Taxes, *Forbes*, February 28, 2013, www.forbes.com.

Brewster, Scott, "Money Pros: How to Choose between a UGMA/UTMA and a 529 Plan When Picking a College Savings Tool," *New York Daily News*, June 20, 2014, www.nydailynews.com.

"Can Grandparents Buy EE Savings Bonds for Their Grandchildren's Education?" Finance, Zacks, May 18, 2018, www.finance.zacks.com.

Clark, Ken, "Beginner's Guide to UGMA and UTMA Custodial Accounts," Saving for College, The Balance, March 26, 2018, www.thebalance.com.

"Education Planning," Treasury Direct, 2018, www.trwasurydirect.gov.

"Frequently Asked Questions About Coverdell Education Savings Accounts," Investment Company Institute, 2018, www.ici.org.

Hurley, Joseph, *The Best Way to Save for College – A Complete Guide to 529 Plans*, Savingforcollege.com Publications, Pittsford, New York, 2015, www.savingforcollege.com.

Kantrowitz, Mark, "Rolling US Savings Bonds into a 529 College Savings Plan for Tax-Free Treatment" Fastweb, July 30, 2012, www.fastweb.com.

Lankford, Kimberly, "Using Savings Bonds to Pay College Costs," Ask Kim, *Kiplinger*, July 13, 2012, www.kiplinger.com.

Powell, Farran, "5 Things to Know About Using an IRA to Pay for Tuition – A Roth Individual Retirement Account is an Alternative Way to Help Pay for Higher Education Expenses," *US News & World Report*, March 30, 2016, www.usnews.com.

"Requirements for Using Savings Bonds for College Expenses," Personal Finance, College Savings, Dummies, www.dummies.com.

"Retirement Plans and Saving for College," FinAid, www.finaid.org.

"Series I Savings Bonds," 2018, www.savingsbonds.com.

"Should Parents Transfer College Savings from an UTMA Account to a 529 Plan?" Fastweb, August 28, 2017, www.fastweb.com.

"Tax Cuts and Jobs Act: Overview of Provisions that Sunset (Expire)," News Special Publications Tax, Maxwell, Locke & Ritter, January 11, 2018, www.mlrpc.com.

"Thinking About using Your Retirement Savings to Pay for College? Think Again," Fidelity Learning Center, www.fidelity.com.

"UGMA & UTMA Custodial Accounts," FinAid, www.finaid.org.

"Using Savings Bonds for Education," FS Publication 0051, Bureau of the Fiscal Services, Department of the Treasury, July 2015, www.treasurydirect.gov.

Williams, Andrea, "3 Big Differences Between 529 College Savings Plans, UTMA Accounts," *US News & World Report*, July 29, 2015, www.usnews.com.

Wikipedia, "Coverdell Education Savings Account," www.wikipedia.com.

Ziff, Deborah, "Pros, Cons of Paying for College with Savings Bonds," Education, *US News & World Report*, February 1, 2017, www.usnews.com.

CHAPTER 19 – ESTATE PLANNING ISSUES

"529 Plans and Estate Planning," Broadridge Investor Communications Solutions, www.aicpa.org.

"A 529 Plan Can Benefit Your Estate Plan," Adler Pollock & Sheehan, PC, August 4, 2017, www.jdsupra.com.

"Another Estate Planning Tool: The 529 Plan," Wealth Management, Mercer Advisors, November 15, 2016, www.merceradvisors.com.

Beyond Educational Savings-Gifting and Estate Planning with 529 Plans, Boston: Columbia Management Distributors, 2009.

Bischoff, Bill, "Using 529 College Savings Accounts for Estate Planning," MarketWatch, October 7, 2014, www.marketwatch.com.

Cullen, Terri, "Potential Pitfalls of 529 Plans When Priority Isn't College," Fiscally Fit, *The Wall Street Journal*, January 23, 2003, www.wsj.com.

Ebeling, Ashlea, "Trusts in the Age of Trump: Time to Re-Engineer Your Estate Plan," Personal Finance, *Forbes*, February 13, 2018.

Ebeling, Ashlea, "Where Not to Die in 2018," Personal Finance, *Forbes*, December 21, 2017, www.forbes.com.

"Estate Planning and 529 Plans," Research & Insights, Ameriprise Financial, www.ameriprise.com.

"Estate Tax Tables," Washington Department of Revenue, 2018, www.dor. wa.gov.

Hurley, Joseph, "Naming Successor of Grandparent's 529 Plan," Student Loans, Bankrate, January 11, 2010, www.bankrate.com.

McCabe, David J.; Posner, David J.; "2018 Estate, Gift and GST Tax Exemption Increases and Increase in the Annual Gift Tax Exclusion," Wilkie Farr & Gallagher, December 27, 2017, www.willkie.com.

O'Connor, Brian J., "Heirs Inherit Uncertainty with New Estate Tax," *The New York Times*, February 23, 2018, www.nytimes.com.

Sheedy, Rachel L., "State Death Taxes Losing Life," Estate Planning, *Kiplinger's Retirement Report*, January 2017, www.kiplinger.com.

"State Death Tax Chart," The American College of Trust and Estate Counsel, June 14, 2018, www.actec.org.

"Using 529 Plans to Invest for College and Transfer Wealth," Merrill Edge, Bank of America, 2018, www.merrilledge.com.

Walczak, Jared, *State Inheritance and Estate Taxes: Rates, Economic Implications and the Return of Interstate Competition*, Washington DC: Tax Foundation, July 17, 2017.

"Who Controls the 529 Account if the Owner Dies?" Wealthfront, May 27, 2018, www.support.wealthfront.com.

CHAPTER 20 – CREATING AN EDUCATIONAL FAMILY DYNASTY

Cornell Law School, "U.S. Code, Title 26, Subtitle F, Chapter 79, 7710 – Definitions," Legal Information Institute, www.law.cornell.edu.

Hurley, Joseph, "Choosing a Successor Account Owner," Savingforcollege.com, March 27, 2008, www.savingforcollege.com.

"Legal Disclosures," Ohio Tuition Trust Authority, College Advantage, Ohio's 529 Savings Program, April 6, 2015, www.collegeadvantage.com.

"Michigan 529 Advisor Plan Disclosure Booklet and Participation Agreement," The Michigan Department of the Treasury, September 11, 2017, www.Mi529advisor.com.

"New York's 529 College Savings Program, Direct Plan Online," New York's 529 College Savings Program, November 18, 2017, www.nyckidsrise.org.

"PA 529–Guaranteed Savings Plan Disclosure Statement," Pennsylvania Treasury, March 2018, www.pa529.com.

"What is the Seventh Generation Principle," Working Effectively with Indigenous Peoples, Indigenous Corporate Training, Inc., May 29, 2012, www.ictinc.ca.

INDEX

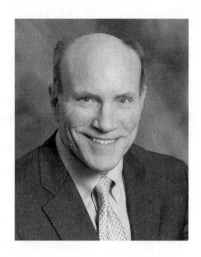

ABOUT THE AUTHOR

For thirty-five years, Jeff Pritchard has worked with some of the nation's premier wealth management organizations, advising families how to achieve their multigenerational financial and philanthropic goals. Jeff holds a master of business administration degree (MBA) and is a certified financial planner (CFP) and a chartered advisor in philanthropy (CAP).

He is the author of five other books and has been quoted in publications, such as *US News & World Report, Trusts & Estates, Money,* and *USA Today.*